Fast Pitch
Fifties

To order additional copies of this book, contact:
Xlibris Corporation
1-888-795-4274
www.Xlibris.com
Orders@Xlibris.com
132242

Dedicated to

GEORGE GALLO

POPEYE NINE

Christmas Present

Our Christmas tree in the 50s was silver, a W.T. Grant model #205317, which I easily recall because the model number included Mom's favorite number to "play." She believed, like other folks at that time, the number came from above like an opportunistic message to figure out. Anyway, the tree had its advantages - it didn't shed any pine needles, was easily put away, and was short enough to not stretch too far to put the star on the top.

Except for Mom, she needed a stool...

Expectations for Christmas presents were dictated by Dad's insistence no gift be any bigger than what you could fit in a pocket. It was a very practical way of doing things. And it made things all somewhat easier to figure out: no shiny new Buicks parked in front of the house. And for me: no bicycle, yet again this year.

I got used to thinking of different things to do with Venus Paradise color pencils, 100 plastic soldiers as advertised on a comic book's back page, and a game inspired by Howard Garis' "Uncle Wiggily." That aside, this particular Christmas was somewhat different. Our home in New Rochelle felt empty without my older brother. George was in the Army. He always came up with something to make Christmas more festive. But he wasn't around this year.

During the past summer, George had taught me how to keep score of a baseball game, using a blank sheet of paper and a pencil. One evening in the summer, with the scheduled umpire unable to make the game, the home plate ump asked for a "volunteer." And so my career as a baseball scorecard keeper began in earnest. Whenever I could, I'd keep score - on TV games too.

Later that same Christmas, with my brother far away, two of George's friends stopped by to wish us Merry Christmas. One carried a special gift, which George had requested he get for me. To my surprise, it was something I had never seen before. It was an official scorecard book full of preprinted pages with baseball diamonds ready for score keeping from Allen Sports Shop. In his own way, George had remembered me and knew I'd have fun with it.

Now it's my turn, in a small way, to remember him .

- Pete Gallo, Christmas 2012

Introduction: Era of Classics

In a book about history, even a very specific slice of 1950s sports history, there is a point worth making at the beginning. In America, the term nostalgia is not a matter of saying the era I grew up in was simpler, better and more optimistic than yours. It's about "feeling" that it really was and then trying to do the impossible and explain exactly why.

Let us dare to do just that...

Nothing is American as "Baseball, Hot Dogs, Apple Pie and Chevrolet." Or so the 1974 commercial jingle went. In a book about baseball this makes for a pleasant cultural reference that few would challenge. And as clichés go, this Chevrolet television jingle was enduringly memorable largely because it had the merit of being true. Well, I say "true, " in part, because there is no question that baseball, apple pie and even hot dogs have remained enduring icons of Americana for at least two centuries, now entering their third.

But ask yourself this: What about Chevrolet – is there nothing as All-American as a Chevrolet? That remains debatable. To my mind. it depends on the era you are talking about.

After all, not all Chevy models were classics. The 1957 Chevy, however, made an enduring impression on the world. Though it offered less utility and one-one-hundredth of the mileage of today's Chevy Volt, how can one even begin to estimate how inspiring this classic icon both was -- and remains.

Introduction: American Pie

When it comes to summing up feelings of losing 1950s innocence, no one did it better than one famous singer who grew up in the All-American town where much of this book's action transpires – musician Don McLean of New Rochelle.

McLean's chart-topping American Pie, released in 1971 at the height of the Vietnam conflict, remains one of the most enigmatic compositions of American pop culture. It has many interpretations.

Its fame pivots on a cultural inflection point. As many see it, the ballad deals with a gradual changeover in our culture from the optimism of the 1950s to the challenged value systems of the 1960s and beyond.

That premise remains debatable to some, but what isn't debatable is that sentiments expressed in "American Pie" were shared by many who grew up in that era and felt a sense of loss.

For some, the song sounds like a lament. To the those of the younger a generation, it might even sound like a ballad about "good ole' days" that never really existed. And who might blame such ignorance given that what was arguably best about the 1950s was unabashed positive feelings about the future, ourselves, the world and our place in it?

Such cultural ideas defy simple explanation or illustration, yet an entire generation knew them to be and witnessed them slipping away.

In American Pie, McLean does his best to explain the loss in symbolic terms. The song writer channels the demise of Buddy Holly whose music personified hopefulness and a positive spirit as a symbol of a fallen American dream. The perception was that the 1950s, one of the golden ages in U.S. history, had devolved into its historical opposite. From a period of great prosperity in which the nation basked in the sunshine of the hard won allied victory in World War II to the era of bad decisions: Vietnam, and waxing social upheaval.

America reshaped itself and not always for the better or without great pain.

Holly's death in a plane crash in February 1959 was clearly a McLean's metaphor for the "end of the 1950s," both musically and culturally.

Introduction: Fast-pitch Era

Will historians agree the 1950s rocked before it rolled off? Probably. More than any post-war period, the 1950s allowed Americans to fully enjoy the fruits of their individual labor. It had a verifiable tangibility. Americans demanded new suburban homes, new autos and more. And prosperity allowed for more personal time, not just material abundance.

The rise of local sports teams across Main Street, USA was part of all this. In fact, having the time to play recreational sports itself was part of this boom.

In this era, fast-pitch softball rose to unprecedented popularity. America embraced it -- Canada and Cuba, too. Towns, big and small, developed their own homegrown rivalries. Notably, the games were free, smoking was permitted (cigars too), as was eating hotdogs and Italian ices.

Some of this is almost lost to the passage of time. In the context of sports, for instance, windmill play has always been underrated in terms of its popularity and required skill sets. Bowling followed somewhat the same pattern as softball.

McLean's song was right—you can't go home again---but you can recall the many warm memories of the time that passed us - oh so - quickly, and at the same time let future generations know what it was like.

Their story has never been written, but the time has come to tell it - the story of fast-pitch softball in New Rochelle, N.Y. during the 1950s. These "Twilighters" were athletes in every sense of the word. If you were there to see them up close, you would come to appreciate their skills: a batter trying to catch up to a fireballing Danny Brandon or a flashy Jabbo Shelton racing from first to third. You would recall George Gallo's pinpoint throw to catch a base stealer or a feisty Tony Giordano running down a long fly to left center. It was all there and more.

Like their major league counterparts, there were a few players like Cookie Norberto who could knock one into the right field tomato garden at Columbus Field with crack of the pine as could the equally dangerous Turner Stroman. It was all free to watch on a balmy summer evening. Their fields of play had names such as Columbus, Jefferson, Donofrio, and Isaac Young. These were the venues for the Twilight League of the 1950s in the Queen City of the Sound.

Introduction: The Champions Next Door

To get the feel for the teams, players, and characters from that era is the essence of this writing. To understand the unique passion and deep feelings these players felt is to savor the warm summer breezes of the serendipitous fifties.

This book is a "Back to the Future" visit to a period of simple pleasures punctuated by the presence of special people.

The Twilight League was a vestige of the 1940s baseball version which morphed into the populist softball league. This league was populated largely by returning war veterans and a young stable of post high schoolers who skipped college, out of necessity, to work. Softball had been played extensively during the war here and "over there" during free time. At home, it fit nicely into the developing social and economic patterns of the day. That is it required less space, contests were faster-paced than hardball, and moreover you didn't need stadium night lights." Matches ended just after "Twilight Time."

The City of New Rochelle's Recreation Department ran leagues and aimed to keep play competitive. "The Rec" took care of ball fields, set up schedules, and even arbitrated protests.

Each of New Rochelle's fields had distinctive features and topography. Columbus in the summer had the pungent odor of petroleum. Oil was applied at the beginning of each season to keep mini duststorms at bay. D'Onofrio reeked thanks to garbage incinerators fuming nearby. Jefferson had its chain-linked version of Fenway's Green Monster, and Isaac Young had toboggan-ready inclines in the outfield. And there was City Park where you needed a speedy player to cover an outfield expanse that had its own zip code.

Certainly one could make a case for writing a fast-pitch history about other locales in southern Westchester such as Mount Vernon, Mamaroneck, and Yonkers. Of course, Bronx teams fast-pitched, too.

But New Rochelle offers as good an example of the vagaries of fast-pitch softball as any of the aforementioned. And besides it is the most familiar to me as an observer and official scorekeeper of many games. With a remarkable 20 fast-pitch clubs within its tiny 13.2-square mile bounds, New Rochelle in the 1950s was a kind of home base for fast-pitch, you'll come to see. The windmills await...

Introduction: Club House Debates

Fast-pitch softball has a little bit of the cultural allure for which that era would later become famous. The aesthetic feelings which emanated from the mass media mingling of Elvis, Marilyn Monroe and Mickey Mantle comprised the axis of influence for the decade. The good feeling produced from activities and institutions of that era included not just softball but pastimes such as roller skating, professional wrestling, comic books, marbles, double-feature movies, stickball, bowling and many other entertaining pursuits.

The competition for fast-pitch softball was fierce. The players and managers of the teams usually worked in the area where games took place. They also tended not to take their vacations in the summer months. Those that took time off, stayed local. This was an important factor in the ferocity of the competition. Social contact was inherent. Following a game players would meet at a designated location to talk, dwell on mistakes and exaggerate a key hit.

This kind of unselfconscious camaraderie led to a general respect for one another. While sipping on a coke, a Leewood Concordia "grape" soda or a Schaefer beer, these instant experts could not only make the game's machinations crystal clear, they might begin to solve any of the world's problems in simple straightforward style. Standing to the side of any heated exchange invariably stood Pudaleek nursing a Lucky Strike and taking in the free entertainment. Pudaleek was Popeye Nine coach Clap's constant companion. No one knew the origin of his moniker-not even if it was his first or last name.

Discussions sometimes drifted to solving a political or social problem. One particular decision made on a balmy summer night was that tiny Formosa should invade China and oust the reds. What was interesting was how the talk went from baseball to politics in a "West End" minute. Where was the turning point in the conversation that led to a wild transition? Maybe it was the presence on most corners of an older person who had some experience in WW II, and saw a semblance between political power and softball. But the point is that people talked. And whether they had a point or not, there was a venue to say their piece and defend their position with peers. Call it a rustic kind of democracy in action, and it was

Introduction: A Lasting Legacy

Amazingly, local pundits got it right. Looking back fifty or more years, those corner discussion groups correctly predicted the crumbling of communist regimes once their citizenry tasted the fruits of freedom. Mickey Circelli, a player from Seventh Street, proclaimed prisoners in captive nations would riot once they saw Marilyn Monroe in the raw.

The softball leagues were a microcosm of 1950s cross-sectioned society. For example, the Royals, one of the consistently winning teams of the decade were mainly black with a couple of white players. The Popeye Nine were young men from West New Rochelle. Tectape's roster was comprised of local factory employees. And the Bonefero Club was a mix of young and older ballplayers from a social club whose antecedents came from a little town in southern Italy. It was an interesting mix of suburbanites, a melting pot for baseball.

What remains now are scant paper-and-ink newspaper accounts of what transpired during those years of fast-pitch play in New Rochelle.

This book is intended to bring images of era back to life - capturing the real people, vivid emotions and worthy memories of the Twilight League at its height.

1950

Fast Pitches

Twilight League
New Rochelle Embarks on a New Era in Sports History

1950:

World War II was not a distant memory in 1950. It was a scant five years since America poured its emotions into the spacious caverns of Times Square on VE Day to celebrate the end of the great conflict. It would be decades before most of the war stories would find their way into the movie theaters, books and magazines, and finally television. For now, it was usually discussion material at dinner tables and family get-togethers.

Prelude to Play

On the ball fields of New Rochelle, games sometimes pitted WWII vets against current Korean War veterans as well as recent school graduates. This helped launch a decade of highly charged competition in fast-pitch softball. The historic positioning of different groups added to the interest as these were men ready for serious games and championship trophies. We will look at the competition, year by year, starting in 1950, chronicling an amazing ten years unlike any before or since in New Rochelle.

MEMORIAL DAY HERALDS START OF TWILIGHT LEAGUE PLAY

In 1950, New Rochelle geared up its Memorial Day parade festivities with marchers following a North Avenue route to City Hall. Trinity Church hosted ceremonies headed by Mayor Stanley Church and Grand Marshall John Brody. Rabbi Shankman participated in a benediction, and a ceremony was held at Hudson Park for those lost at sea. Awards were also given to those children with the best-decorated bicycles. As expected, war-themed movies dominated the landscape. RKO theater in New Rochelle was showing "Destination Tokyo" starring John Garfield and Cary Grant. And Loews screened Bing Crosby in "Riding High."

One-Armed Marino Pitches a Royal Victory

Chances are you didn't see the ball until it was too late

50

The most valuable player of 1950 Twilight League Season play was someone you would never have guessed. He was Bill Marino, a young man who had suffered an excruciating injury a few years earlier while serving in the U.S. armed forces in World War II. A native of New Rochelle, Marino had always been an avid ball player, and was known before the war as a man who would throw a killer change-up that could strike out a starting line-up in short order. But that was before the war. Now, as the spring of 1950 approached, some of his peers wondered if Marino was still king of the mound.

There was plenty of reason for doubt. After all, Marino had lost his left arm in the war. Some thought he would never play again. But these critics didn't know Marino. A wine salesman by trade, he spent hours a day strengthening his surviving right arm by throwing fast pitches and building up coordination so that he could effectively swing a bat to the point that he was an above-average hitter. He practiced, down the road from his home, at a place called Columbus Field and then would often resume practice again, in private, listening to Frank Sinatra albums on a record player in his backyard.

If players and fans were as incredulous as family and friends about his agility, they chose quietly marvel at his skill rather than draw attention to the obvious. This spoke volumes about the camaraderie shared between teammates and rivals alike in those days. But no one could doubt his abilities once they saw him unleash a fastball.

It was fascinating to see Marino deliver pitches that might exceed 100 miles –per-hour and then suddenly switch to his glove, in one swoop motion, to halt a bunted ball from a hapless batter who had sorely underestimated the speed of his responsiveness on the mound. It took special skill, but Marino had taken the time to develop and hone that skill with devastating exactness.

His handicap didn't draw as much attention back then as it might today. Coverage in the local newspaper only mentioned him being "armless." Single-armed pitchers were few and far between. But Marino didn't just play. He excelled to the point that he was considered, locally, a Peter Gray of the Twilight League.

Quicker than Even the Big Leagues

A good pitcher could decide not only a game, but the season.

For those of you too young to remember, Gray was the one-armed outfielder for the St. Louis Browns in that era. Gray was surprisingly adept with a bat.

Marino was also a dexterous swinger. But for fast-pitch softball, there was a difference to note. Whereas the average hardball thrown by a big league pitcher might register anywhere from 75 miles per hour or higher, fast-pitch softballs thrown by wizards like Marino were faster still – coming at speeds of 85 miles-per-hour or better.

This put fast-pitch softball in a league of its own. Pitches buzzing over the plate at speeds 20 percent faster than those seen in the major leagues are simply more difficult to hit. So it's no surprise that fast-pitch softball was a sport where pitchers were often the determinant not only of who won a given game but which team would sweep a season.

A regular hardball is easier to see coming at you, over the batter's box. But the windmill motion in softball obscures exactly when the pitched is released, making timing simply difficult for a batter.

One pitch more prominent in softball than hardball is the riser,

which handcuffs a batter because it heads above their standard wheelhouse, the swing pattern that roughly arcs - outward and upward - from a player's waist.

This fit Marino's style. Off the field, he could be stubborn and resolute. He was willing to speak his mind.

Although, he started the season as a number-two pitcher for his team, he was determined to win. He grew up and lived in the predominately Italian-American neighborhood of West New Rochelle, but Marino joined a more veteran team that was formed in the 1940s called the Royals that boasted a roster that was made up of mainly black players from the adjacent Remington Place neighborhood.

A veteran team in both senses of the word, Royals were both slightly older and many served together in World War II.

The Royals were the perennial favorites amongst teams playing in the three divisions of fast-pitch softball organized by the New Rochelle Recreation Department. These three divisions came under the umbrella name Twilight League.

Early Season
Winding the Windmill at City Park

50

Marino played to win and proved a workhouse for the Royals in the 1950 Season and beyond. Marino thrived and performed best in high-pressure situations.

His trademark was throwing a change-up that befuddled batters. Good curves and an above-average fastball were also in his arsenal. His style contrasted the classic hardball power pitcher of that era who would blast the ball across the plate before you saw it, sometimes with little finesse.

An early indicator of Marino's strength in 1950 came when shut out the Forresters, 4 to 0.

Later, an injury on the roster would leave Marino with a pivotal pitching role during the final showdown of the season's championship series.

But Marino wasn't the only fast thrower in the league, not even on his own team. The Royals ace pitcher was Bobby Simmons who was a more typical of the star hurlers of that era. Simmons opened the first game of the 1950s fast-pitch in New Rochelle with a blaze of bullets.

The season began at New Rochelle's City Park, a sprawling but flat 20-acre parcel that was home to four baseball diamonds -- three set aside for fast-pitch softball with games often played simultaneously. The Memorial Day opener saw the Royals face an upstart club sponsored by the American Legion. Joe Sharkey did his best to hold the team in check. But at the end of seven innings he had been out duelled by Simmons. The Royals won with a final a score of 4 to 1.

The Royals would continue that winning streak on their path to the playoffs.

Meanwhile, other early action in the 1950s season showed that hitters could turn the tide against some of the best fast-throwers. For instance, "Pop" Papalardo put the Upsetters ahead early in the season by finishing off the South Side Boys Club with a key hit.

The Curlers, another of the league's veteran teams dating from the 1940s, in their 1950 opener rode Ed Amori's bat to a victory over the Rangers, 2 to 0.

TV personality Jay Leno was born in New Rochelle on April 28, 1950

The Rangers would strike back hard, crushing the Centre Streeters 8 to 1 with the help of Len Piedmont's two base hits. Piedmont was a good-hitting pitcher who had no trouble getting on base with the swing of his bat.

As the season progressed, the more experienced teams who often boasted the best pitchers broke away from the pack. While the Royals continued unbeaten, the Rangers occupied first place.

The Mapmen, a team sponsored by local cartography shop, were the surprise of the Industrial Division that year, rising in early season play.

Another team, the Bonefro Club edged the Whirls when catcher named "Bavac" provided

In 1950, Twilight softball games were covered in the local paper with a bare minimum of ink. Results were simply stated, if reported at all. Commentary was practically nil. The reader was expected to read between the lines of the box score.

Bonnies, Burigo and B-Ball

The Bonefro Club, a bastion of local talent, would produce another unexpected win that would inspire players throughout the league. Early in the 1950 Season, third-baseman Sil Burigo of the "Bonnies" was signed to the minor league ball club, the Bristol Owls, a Bristol, Conn.-based B-Ball club. When he was scouted Burigo was playing in New Rochelle as well as for the Fordham University team in the Bronx. The "Bonnies" proved itself one of the "franchise" teams in the Twilight League, usually contending for honors each season. Over the years, their stable of players were second to none. There was pitcher Len Piedmont. Other players were Sonny Funicello, the Connolly brothers, Vin and Joe as well as Bert Terranova, Donald Summo, and Joe DiBuono, John and Pat Mandarano. Notables also included Jake Cassara, Sal Sclafani, and Joe Sheehan. The Bonefro name emanated from the tiny mountain town nestled in the Italian province of Compasso. In the early twentieth century, residents emigrated to New Rochelle where they set up a social club that become avid sponsors of local softball teams.

On Sale in New Rochelle in 1950

Liggett's Drugstore	Carton of Lucky Strikes	- $1.69
Wolfson's	Living room furniture set	- $49.00
The London Shop	Men's cotton pajamas	- $2.95
Gale's Army Navy	Men's belt	- .95

Post Season Play

To everyone's surprise, the Bonnies looked to dethrone the Royals

50

The Twilight League's team roster was so thick that it was organized across three divisions to accommodate schedules and to keep play competitively balanced. The Industrial League was the most senior division with arguably better teams. Its winning club faced off against the winner of the a game between the other two divisions, National and American, in a best of three series for the annual championship.

```
Championship
Lineup for
'ROYALS'
Stroman    1B
Kemp       2B
Thomas     SS
Flowers    3B
Lybrand    LF
Allen      CF
Jannen     RF
Williams   C
Simmons    P
```

In 1950, the intrepid Mapmen captured the Industrial flag. Bonefro Club's Rangers won the National. And the Royals clinched the American pennant.

Bonefro Club in the first of the playoff games shut out the Curlers 5 to 0 as ace Len Piedmont threw goose eggs for Bonefro. In the second confrontation, Piedmont's two hitter decided the National League championship - with a 1 to 0 victory - eliminating the Curlers.

On the American side of Twilight League, the Royals notched the division title with a 5 to 4 win over American Legion's Post-8 team. The Royals won the first game over the Legion, 3 to 2, losing catcher Earl Williams to injury.

```
Championship
Lineup for
'BONNIES'
Giannetti   1B
Terranova   2B
Garry       SS
Vaccaro     3B
Cicere R    LF
Iarocci     CF
Cicere P    RF
Perricone   C
Piedmont    P
```

The stage was set for a Bonefro vs. Royals showdown. The city was excited at the prospect of two of the most talent-laden teams poised to duel. This series sparked unprecedented attention from the public and set the stage for growing interest in local fast-pitch for the rest of the fifties.

The pressure was on coach Bruce Flowers and his champion Royals team. They carried the banner for the older veteran ballplayers, while the Bonefro "Bonnies" largely represented younger South Side upstarts.

The Royals were beset with a key injury. Catcher Earl Williams had been injured in the series with the American Legion. Manager Bruce Flowers was forced to start his ace pitcher Bob Simmons as catcher.

Even so, the Royals were still slight favorites to win. But Bonefro went about their business and struck first. They surprised the Royals, winning 4 to 2, to go up one game to none. It was Len Piedmont's skillful pitching that held the Royals to five hits And Bert Terranova's clutch hitting keyed the Bonnies' win. The Bonefro Club was just one game away...

In Game Two of the 1950 Series, the Royals struck with a vengeance. With Bobby Simmons on the mound, the Royals bombarded the Bonnies, 10 to 3, evening up the series. Two Royals, Brud Flowers and Steve Kemp , each recorded 3 for 3 in the batting ledger.

The 1950 Season whittled down to one dramatic out. At City Park, the game was nip and tuck with Marino on the mound for the Royals in the bottom of the sixth. It was getting dark and chances were good this would be the last inning. Royals held the lead 6 to 5. Across the other side of City Park, the semi-pro New Rochelle Bulldogs were grinding into shape for the upcoming football season while the Royals and Bonnies were pulling the curtain closed on theirs. The Bonnies had managed to get two men on base with two outs. The entire season hung in the balance.

Bruce Flowers anxiously visited his moundsman, Bill Marino, who held the softball on his left side and listened to Flowers say a few words and pat him on the back. Marino who had been down this road many times before, stepped on the rubber and nodded in agreement with a sign from the catcher, Bob Simmons. The Bonefro runners each stood perched on their bases, first and second, ready to fly. Marino delivered, and the Bonnies batter Perricone went for the first pitch. He hit it solidly towards left-center but left fielder Lybrand moved towards the gap to snare the ball. Fans streamed onto the field to congratulate Marino and the Royals team. It had not been easy, but the Royals were champs, again. For Marino, it was another triumphal comeback. Earlier, he had lost his left arm to enemy shrapnel and rehabbed a period of years. Like other veterans on his team, his steely nerves had been through the fire, on and off the field. The Royals, a club that had come of age in the 40s, now entered a new decade as champions.

The Great Jewel Robber

A film called the "Great Jewel Robber" based on the notorious life of Gerard Dennis of New Rochelle had its world premiere in June. Mayor Stanley Church Played himself in the movie. Marjorie Reynolds and David Brian starred in the flick, which was produced by Bryan Foy, member of a famous New Rochelle family.

1951

New Rochelle's
Talk of the Town

1951

The 38th Parallel

In 1951, the United States was coming to grips with the Korean conflict and a booming national economy that boosted demand for schools, highways, and hospitals to accommodate growth. Ed Sullivan was emceeing American cultural change, live on-air. Cinemas feared TV would put them out of business. Print media of all kinds flourished, and the NY Daily News sunday edition sold 4 million copies.

Homer Heard Around the World

Bobby Thomson, without question, saved the year. Hitting the shot heard round the world gave the New York Giants a miracle comeback to win the pennant over the Brooklyn Dodgers, adding a national glow and a timeless memory that still stands out in baseball history. Coogan's Bluff was the site of the Giants come back from a 13-game deficit.

"N-E-Two" and the Rotary Revolution

It was during the summer of 1951 that the "NE-2" telephone exchange arrived in New Rochelle. The newest 'rage' was called "rotary dialing,"and it allowed you to place calls directly. Days of picking up a phone and waiting for an operator to plug your call in via a switchboard that began in 1892 had come to an end. "Party lines" would persist for some time. But modern 1950s convenience had arrived for NE-Two.

DRAG RACING OFF NORTH AVENUE

In a scene that could have served as inspiration for James Dean's "Rebel without a Cause," New Rochelle residents in the Rochelle Park area called police to stop wild teenagers from riding souped-up cars at 75 miles-an-hour on a nearby grassy plain and terrorizing local squares, Daddy-O's and other standerbys. Judge Thomas Fasso reprimanded the teens, ordering a them to cease and desist.

Where is West New Rochelle?

Baseball, Zeppole and Lemon Ice

West New Rochelle was not a place you could find indexed in an atlas, or listed on a map of New York State. Technically it did not exist at all, nor does it now. Still, don't tell that to the tens of thousands of West Enders who lived there in the 1950s. For them, "The West" was a state of mind. These included many second-generation Americans, then in their teens, whose parents most likely arrived via boat to Ellis Island from far off lands half a century earlier. Many of these older immigrants, with their own hands, helped transform West New Rochelle from a sleepy residential enclave south of the Main Street District into a bustling quasi-Italian paese full of bakeries, ethnic food markets and unexpected volume of light industry kept ever busy amidst a post-War building boom.

Gathering at St. Joseph's Church in New Rochelle was a big deal in 1951 for those celebrating the feast of St. Anthony of Padua, a priest from the 12th century, follower of St. Francis of Assisi, and patron saint of lost items, missing people, and for some -- lost baseball teams, like the then struggling Giants.

For many who attended the weekend of festivities, it wasn't St. Anthony or his statue which occupied the northeast corner of the school playground that got their attention. It was the overwhelming bouquet of sausage and onions meeting the equally potent aroma of zeppole that charged the atmosphere.

The orchestra played brass-heavy Italian favorites on a bandstand. Children scooted underneath a red, white and blue bunting covering the bandstand to cross to the far side of the playground. An elderly man urged you to take a chance on a 1951 Cadillac. And young men tried to prove their mettle by climbing a greasy pole with little success. The pole was slicked with oil and was very difficult to climb. Awards for reaching the top ranged from church blessings to cash prizes.

The greasy pole challenge looked easy at first, but required a lot of sweat, and tenacity.

A curiosity, it certainly was not a team sport. Instead, the young men of the West End looked to baseball as their pastime.

May brought the start of Twilight League fast-pitch play. By June 12, the day of the feast, the 1951 Season was already getting interesting.

Norberto's Brazen Swings

Batting legends inspired fear even amongst top-tier pitching clubs

51

Fast-pitches careening over the plate at 100 miles per hour may have been a trademark of mercenaries of the mound in 1950s Twilight play. But the best batters of the era, a select few, rose to the challenge and became legends in their own right. Such men inspired fear even amongst top-tier pitching clubs.

One of these was West New Rochelle's Cookie Norberto who proved his mettle in the 1951 Season. Fans, teammates and foes alike considered Norberto one of the Twilight Leagues most dangerous hitters – and rightly so. He had a compact swing that would allow him to lead the league in home runs in 1951 and for much of the decade.

Norberto was so adept with a stick that it was not unheard for him to "out bat" the entire line-up of his own team combined in a given game or even series.

Throughout the decade, he would play for a number of clubs including Popeye Nine, Tectape , Warrens and even the perennial champs, the Royals.

He was sought after for semiannual tournament games played at Sanford Boulevard in Mount Vernon, where teams from neighbouring towns like Mamaroneck would come to challenge visiting clubs from as far away as Peekskill.

A natural all-star, he also imagined he could do a better job than the assigned umpires. Norberto didn't shy away from telling umps when he thought their calls were just plain wrong.

Even people who didn't attend Twilight games would come to learn Norberto's name as his signature homers came crashing onto neighbouring homes, through windows and into gardens like that of Mr. Esposito whose tomato patch lay just beyond center right at Columbus Field in New Rochelle.

Norberto would take his slugger persona off field too, mostly to amuse friends who knew he was really a congenial guy. Though short and compact, a tattoo-wearing Norberto liked to stir things up. Friends recall him and fellow players making a roadside stop at a motel in Connecticut to catch a televised Giants football game and then adopting New York tough talk to inspire the manager to climb up on the roof and play with the aerial when transmission was lost after kickoff.

Upstart Gotti's Aim for the Throne
Fourteen-Consecutive Wins on the Way to a Title

In 1951, Norberto played for the Scorpions, an underdog club that would not make it into the finals despite Norberto's prodigious swing. Actually there were dual Norbertos playing for the Scorpions that year. The other was his brother Frank.

The 1951 Twilight League Season kicked off with the Scorpions taking on 'Wanaque Athletic Club,' whose name referred to fictitious sports club located somewhere in 'West New Rochelle,' itself a made up name. Not surprisingly, the Norbertos led the Scorpions to victory with a 4-for-4 batting mark by Frank and a line-drive homer from Cookie. Jerry Hempfield of Wanaque would prove a good hitter for this club, whose players would later form another fast-pitch club called the Popeye Nine.

As the 1951 Season progressed, it became apparent that an upstart club called the Gotti Nine would be in contention for the championship against an emerging dynasty, the Royals who in 1951 had their eye on their sixth-consecutive championship win for New Rochelle's Twilight League.

The Royals remained a devastating force to consider. In one game, pitcher Bill Marino of the Royals had little trouble scattering five hits to beat the Rangers, 14 to 1.

Some may have attributed this to poorer play from the Rangers since another veteran team, the Bonefro Club capitalized on the bats of Joe Sheehan and Chip Esposito to edge out the Rangers in early season as well.

As good as the Royals were, games remained highly contested in 1951. For instance, although the Royals managed to defeat New Rochelle's American Legion team, 3 to 1, pitcher Bob Becker of the Legion held the Royals to a paltry four hits. And the results might have been different, if C. Thomas of the Royals had not succeeded in sparking a rally with a crack double. This kept the Royals on a trajectory to win the championship for the league.

Poker and B-Ball

Friendly wagering was not talked about much in those days. The early 50s saw a crackdown in illegal gambling that erupted in local scandals that included elected Tuckahoe officials being convicted of permitting poker games catering to NYC bookies.

Of Empires, Bonnies and Royals
Twilight League playoffs draw increasing fervor

If the Royals' stats looked increasingly impressive, then so did that of the Gotti Nine. By a score of 14 to 3, the Gotti Nine blasted the Forresters and extended their winning streak to ten games. Homers against the Forresters came from Gotti's "Kid" St. John and Bob Vanderslice.

With the second round of post-season play dwindling down in the National Division, the Gotti Nine had aimed to hold onto a runaway momentum.

Some fans thought 1951 might belong to the Bonefro club. That changed when the Bonnies met the Royals on-field for the first time that season. The Royals relentlessly capitalized on Bonnies' errors, winning 9 to 3. What helped most was Royals first baseman Turner Stroman clearing the decks with a double. The Bonnies' best moment in the showdown came with Vin Connolly's two hits, off of Royals' ace Bobby Simmons.

Round Two:

A debate about who might emerge the season's champs was discussed not only by Twilight League players themselves, but by regular residents to a degree that might be hard to fathom today. From barber shop debates to local sports pages, New Rochelleans treated fast-pitch softball play not just as recreation but as something akin to hosting a minor league baseball franchise.

As early as 1951, a period when Twilight League was just beginning to grow in popularity, championship series showdowns were already drawing in hundreds of spectators – a figure that would grow to thousands by the second half of the decade.

As the playoffs commenced, fans and casual observers eagerly went about handicapping the odds or simply building up their favorite teams to justify their pick.

The Royals, the reigning champs, were the easy favorite. They had a balanced offense and the most experience.

Bonefro boasted good pitching, deeper and more impressive than most.

New Rochelle's Fort Slocum team was a longshot with solid batting but barely adequate pitching. Others liked the Forresters who struck a balance between a good offense and a capable defense.

Momentum Ends for Gotti Nine

After an amazing win streak, it was tough way to lose

Meanwhile, the Gotti Nine had a hard hitting lineup, but some defensive concerns marked by a shallower depth of pitching talent.

But the Gotti Nine's pitcher John Benevento would help lead the team to victory, bringing them into post-season play with a simply remarkable twelve-consecutive-winning games.

Royals vs. Gotti Nine

The playoff for a division title brought the Gotti Nine head to head with the Forresters for a best-of-three matchup.

Following a scoreless draw in their first game, the Gotti Nine, helped by Benevento's strong showing that allowed just four hits, subdued the Forresters, 6 to 3.

In the third game of the series, shortstop St. John garnered three hits for Gotti's and scored three times from his leadoff position, allowing the Gotti Nine to crush the Forresters in a blowout.

The Gotti's now boasted an impressive 14-game winning streak.

In a best-of-three series to determine the eventual softball

The Gotti's now boasted an impressive 14-game winning streak.

championship of New Rochelle, the Royals made short work of the Gotti Nine in the opener. The result of the first contest was a 10-to-2 final in favor of the Royals that, once again, Bill Marino helped fashion. On offense, the Royals outclassed Gotti pitching led by Benevento, that gave up ten hits in a matchup that was more lopsided than most fans expected.

Game Two was key for Gotti's. Could they manage a comeback against the Royals?

The answer was a resounding "no." When workhorse Bill Marino took the mound for the Royals, he threw an almost flawless game. On the scoreboard, it was nothing but goose eggs for the Gotti Nine who were vanquished by the Royals, 7 to zip.

After an amazing win streak in regular play, it was a tough way to end a season.

High Noon at City Park
A Flowering of a Royal Dynasty

51

Meanwhile, in the Industrial league playoffs, the Empires swept the title.

The Empires had beaten the Snappies, 11 to 4. And led by Lefty Immediato's pitching they earned a win against the FireCops, 9 to 5. The Empires' Bob Green helped clinch the division title with an imperious homer. So as the late summer series arrived, it would be the Empires against the Royals.

Royals take on the Empires

In the first game of the series, Bobby Simmons squared off against Bob Fuerst of the Empires. The crowd of about 300 was disappointed as the Royals won in a rout, 8 to 0. To top things off, Simmons allowed no hits.

The Royals were one more victory away from their sixth-straight title victory.

Following a rocky start, where Bill Marino yielded two runs to Empire, the Royals rebounded with Bruce Flower's four run-producing base hits. By defeating the Empires 7 to 2, the Royals wrapped up another championship.

It was as if Bruce Flowers of the Royals had read the script of High Noon, a classic film released that same year. Like star Gary Cooper, playing an uncompromising sheriff in an obscure town, Flower's steady performance helped overcome what seemed considerable odds. Though things looked uphill at the onset of post-season, the fast guns of Marino and Simmons turned the tide for these unsung heroes of the day.

1952

Vignettes
from around town

1952

Ike 'Likes' New Rochelle

Presidential pomp came to New Rochelle in 1952. It was Dwight Eisenhower against Adlai Stevenson for the chief executive spot. Westchester County was considered up for grabs. So politicking was fierce. Stevenson promised a visit in August. Ike, refusing to be outdone, decided to make a stop in New Rochelle (and apparently every other town that could be reached by train in the area).

Like others, I recall catching a glimpse of "Ike" at the New Rochelle train station. In a special train headed southbound to Grand Central Station, he spoke briefly from the last car. This was near the Centre Avenue bridge overpass. At that time, my family lived at Washington Avenue before it was divided by New England Thruway construction. I was on Grand Street, which led to the railroad's southbound side, where Mayflower Van Lines was housed. From there, I couldn't hear what Ike said. But I do recall his staff gave out promotional "I Like Ike" buttons. Memorable? Yes, but I recall being more impressed seeing television star William Boyd as "Hopalong Cassidy" at Columbus School soon afterwards.

Women Take the Field

In August 1952, the New Rochelle All Stars captured the first women's softball tourney at Moore Field. The local gals crushed the Shangri-Lulus of Greenwich, 12 to 4. The All Stars, a conglomeration of members from numerous city clubs, eliminated the Mount Vernon entry, 7 to 6. Sis Barton delivered a homerun to break a 6-to-6 tie. Offense was paced by Peg Eustus and Jo Paladino.

ALL AMERICAN

New Rochelle's Johnny Bianco, who resided at Beechwood Avenue, was elected to the All American team by the American Association of College Baseball Coaches this year. He batted .363 as a third baseman in twenty games for the Manhattan College Jaspers and was the only representative of a New York Metro college team to receive the honor. He was a graduate of Albert Leonard High School.

First Season of Little League
New Rochelle Welcomes Tiny Champions

Nowadays, Little League is ubiquitous. But in 1952, it was new. That year, the first season ever in New Rochelle inaugurated what would later become a tradition.

Players were ferried in a parade like fashion in trucks traveling through the downtown en-route to City Park, the new home of local Little League.

In the debut game of the new league, a team called the Rockets blasted the Hornets, 16 to 4. The first homer was hit by pint-sized slugger Frank Miceli.

Controversy abounded. Parents feared tykes would find baseball extremely intense for their young sensibilities. They did, and apparently loved it. Enrollment soared.

The official record keeper, locally, was a man named Norman Ainman who took his job seriously.

He released stats for Little Leaguers at the end of each week. And the newspaper found a way to win over some very young readers with something other than comic strips.

Ainman's early record keeping shows a young Miceli netted the most impressive results in early New Rochelle Little League play.

```
Home Runs

Miceli    Royals    9
Pallet    Eagles    6
Coleman   Hornets   6

Batting

Miceli         .833
Dolce          .600
Brown          .564
Sugahara       .435
```

Signs of the Times
What Advertisers were Pushing in 1952

Looking at local ads in newspapers and on billboards from the Summer of 1952 illustrates changes taking shape in lifestyles, technology and the ever evolving art of marketing.

Ads from the Hi-Lite Photo Shop located on Mechanic Street in New Rochelle touted film development "the same day," as well as the availability of jumbo prints. The world of almost-instant gratification had arrived and it was picture perfect -- or at least you could get a refund on 35-mm prints that didn't make it.

This applied to even things that no one could be sure you needed in the first place, like cigarettes. Camel ads aggressively boasted that its "Turkish-blended" style "leads all others," outselling rival smoke-makers "by billions!" Newspapers and billboard ads went the distance. Some claimed that smoking was even good for honing your voice before a speech. And celebrities attested - it worked! Who could argue with that sort of bold marketing?

Some ads were very serious and show public health concerns for ills that have since, largely, been eradicated. For instance, the Sulllivan Agency at 304 North

Avenue offered "polio insurance policies" that would pay $ 5,000 per year. Polio still menaced millions worldwide.

Ads for vocational schools also promised to get New Rochelleans ready for the jobs of the future. The Berkeley School offered training for private secretaries as demand was picking up in this growth area.

Sears Roebuck & Co. in 1952 was expanding its mail order empire by placing ads for its catalog service just about everywhere, just in case you forgot it had already arrived in the post.

Sears boosted the availability of items in its catalog to a stunning 4,000 products. The catalog was like a department store showroom landing on your kitchen table, and it weighed almost as much.

Cinema ads were also becoming more prevalent. Hollywood studios loved that local theaters footed the bills for ads.

In 1952, films advertised included Abbott & Costello's "Jack and the Beanstalk," Yvonne DeCarlo's "San Francisco Story" and Red Skelton's "Lovely to Look At."

Renaissance Players

You Cover One Position, I'll Take the Other Eight.

In many ways the fast-pitch softball players in the 1950's resembled Dave Philley who played major league ball between 1941 and 1962.

Philley wore only one hat on the field. But he played many different positions in his career -- six to be exact. He was an outstanding defensive player. And was one of baseball 's best clutch hitters. Pinch hitting, he once managed eight-consecutive hits.

Versatility was his edge. Rare in the specialist-centric major leagues, this attribute was a must for Twilight League Players.

In fact, when you signed on to play softball in the Twilight Era, you had to prepare to play any position for any of many possible reasons and be ready to pinch hit. You might start a game on first base but end up as catcher by the seventh inning. There was no one waiting on the bench, and an injury might result in a team with positions uncovered.

Some of the era's most versatile players also rank among the best.

Here is are some of players who mastered the art of covering multiple positions in 1950s Twilight League play.

Vin Connelly who played for Bonefro Club is remembered as a top-notch pitcher as well as an excellent first baseman.

Tut Mandarano of Tectape was a crack hitter. He played all infield and outfield spots as well as catcher. No one knew where he might turn up, next game.

Ron Semenza not only played various positions, he played for multiple squads during his career. He stand out as a strong-armed outfielder, though he covered infield, occasionally, when needed.

Al Ryder was a "Bonnies" memorable who was a solid, rangy, ballplayer. He stinted at shortstop, first base, pitched and caught.

Eddie "Goo Goo" of the Green-Royals-- a gentleman on the field and off -- could credibly play any infield position.

You had to prepare to play any position for any possible contingency

Royal Steamroller Starts Early
An Unbeaten American Legion Ties Royals, Twice!

52

The $64,000 Question facing the rest of the teams in the Twilight League in 1952 was this: Could any club conceivably beat the heavily favored Royals, the regal wrecking crew?

On paper, they looked tough. On field, they were.

Not only were they balanced offensively and defensively. They had excellent pitching, depth, and a lot of experience, up and down the lineup. There were no soft spots.

Just being able to access the Flowers family of ballplayers gave them a distinct advantage. The talented Brud and Ernie Flowers were good pitchers. Brothers Ollie and Al played outfield.

The Royals broke out of the gate, winning nine straight, setting up a key contest with Legion Post 8.

Righty Bill Marino shut out the Cappy's, 12 to 0, backed by a barrage of 13 hits (Lybrand and Shelton each got 3). In other early key games, the Forresters, riding George Pierro's hit, edged the Lucky Nine, 5 to 3.

The Calabria Club outlasted the Red Eyes- 9 to 1 - with Chico Cardenas garnering three hits. Softball veteran Don Summo

hurled and hit the Wanaque to the top of the Community Division with a 10 to 3 victory over the Orioles (a predecessor of the Popeye Nine team.)

The Royals and Post-8 Legionaires, both unbeaten, played two games against each other with the same result: two ties.

The Bonefro Bonnies then rocked the Ringsiders 11 to 3 with star performances turned in by Len Piedmont and AJ Applebaum.

Veteran Woody Woodell won a pitching duel with Bernstein of the Knights 4 to 2.

In the Industrial Division, the "Firemen"tied for first placed at the end of the first round of play with a 6 to 0 shutout of the TeeVees. Bill Sheehan copped the win for the Firemen with a sparkling two hitter.

Scoring four runs in the first inning the Firemen captured the first round of the Industrial Division by beating the Cotlers, 6 to 5. Dick Forst gave up only six hits for the Cotlers as Bob McGuire's hot bat led the Firemen.

A 118-Degree Day is Baseball Weather

Home Plate Melted but the Game Went On...

The headline in the local Standard Star newspaper screamed for attention. The temperature came into town on this early summer day at 118 degrees.

In the evening, Glen Island's bridge jammed from the smothering heat. Traffic lights malfunctioned and cars belched steam and stopped. Hapless workers quit early and heat exhaustion left some suffering. Those seeking relief at city beaches were turned back with a stern warning as if a swarm of sharks had arrived in Echo Bay. Lifeguards simply evacuated, themselves.

Despite the wicked heat, the late-afternoon games went on. At stake were the remaining First Round titles. And the game softball fans were waiting to see most was the American Legion versus the Royals. Both teams were undefeated. It was the matchup of the season so far.

The Royals started Bobby Simmons against the Legion's Joe Sharkey. Taking advantage of the Royals' porous defense, the Legion loaded the bases but Simmons, the Royals pitcher, dodged the bullet by retiring the side with no runs. In the last half of the inning, the Royals knotted the score 3 to 3, when Earl Williams rallied on Richardson's hit to center field.

In the fifth inning, Sil Burigo smacked a double down the left-field line for the Legion. Burigo went to third on a wild pitch and scored on an error.

Now there was a golden opportunity to stack the bases full of Legionaires, but Simmons quashed the momentum. The Legion rally fell short with a harmless pop out.

It was time for the Royals to capitalize. The always dependable Richardson tripled. Next it was Rudy Kemp. He doubled, followed by Neil Richardson's two bagger which brought home the winning run.

Both the Royals and Legion were undefeated, and fans eagerly waited the matchup

Round Two Begins
Lefty Ianuzzi Did Not Allow a Hit

52

In other first-round playoff action, the Forresters nipped the Gotti Nine for the National Division title. After a rocky first frame, Gotti hurler Lefty Ianuzzi did not allow a hit but fortunately for the Forrest men, they scored all their runs in the first inning which was enough to win, 6 to 1. Ozzie Lauer hit a decisive homer for the Forresters.

The Forresters club, located in the city's West End expected an easy win, but the Cappy's reversed the tables in a big upset, 16 to 7, at Moore Field with top performances by vets Terranova and Brescia

As Second Round play began, attention was focused on one of the teams that was always persistent in making it into contention for the championship. That team was the Bonefro Club. Fans felt the Bonnie roster was as good as any in the league. Their ace pitcher Len Piedmont shut down the Red Eyes 4 to 1 to win their second game in Round Two. Other Second Round highlights included Orioles pitcher Pat Dorme's no-hitter against the Wanaque AC, while the Firemen in the Industrial Division continued to roll with a 12 to 1 pounding of the Splicers.

Connolly Stays in the Zone

One of the remarkable achievements of the 1952 Season was Joe Connolly's of the "Bonnies" striking out 18 batters in a win over the Curlers. At one point, this pitcher struck out nine-consecutive batters. Centerfielder Carmine Scoca knocked in all Bonnie runs that day. The Bonefro Club was on a roll.

At City Park, the Royals stepped up the pace by finally stifling the American Legion Post 8 by a score of 4 to 2. The unbeaten Royals were led by Bruce Flowers' three hits. In another surprise, the Curlers, with only four hits, beat the Legion, 8 to 3. Upsets followed. Team 554 caught the Firemen for only their second victory of the season. Further upsets were on their way...

The Problem with Pitchers

After Mid-Season, Upsets were the Norm

52

In a pattern that shows through the 1950's, during the second half of a given season, a greater number of "upsets" occur.

There are many reasons for this. One is that by mid-season, most of the teams were down to one pitcher, forcing teams to rely on his overworked arm. This was usually not the best option.

Alternatively, they could tap an untested moundsman, but this is problematic because he might bring a limited pitch repertoire.

It was also summer. Some players took time off for vacations. Sometimes there were other circumstances.

One player, scheduled to enter the army draft on a Friday breaks a leg sliding into third base at Columbus School on Tuesday. Call it a sort of forced vacation.

Back on the ball field, a day after the Royals won their sixteenth victory in a row, Bonefro won an important game by whipping the Gotti team, 9 to 3. Len Piedmont starred for the Bonnies allowing just one hit, a homer to Henry St. John. Vin Connelly and third Sacker Esposito divided six hits between them.

Over in the Industrial Division, the Loopers outlasted the Pxers, 16 to 9.

The following week, The Bonies and Royals continued their winning ways.

The Royals Behind Simmons three hitter stung the Forresters 6-1 while The Bonnies also registered a win, this time over the Knights 5 to 2.

Connolly went 3-for-4 at bat for Bonefro. Approaching the playoffs, both squads were confident and both were stocked with talent.

The Forresters kicked off the second round of playoffs going up against the Gotti Nine. Powered by the St.John brothers, Gotti's dominated the first contest against Vince Fay. Mustering up only four hits the Gotti's Lefty Ianuzzi kept the Forest men in check- Final: Gotti 6 Forresters 2.

In the second playoff game, Gotti got a gem performance from Ianuzzi once again with a 8 to 0 pasting of the Forresters. Joe Miele's round tripper with Armando Benevento installed the G Men as winners of the National division.

Now all eyes turned towards The Firemen.

Gotti Nine Face the Fire Men

Fred Ianuzzi Pitched a Storm

Next it was the Gotti Nine vs. Firemen. It always seemed during the playoffs with each passing year, one pitcher was hot and performed above his regular season output. In 1952 the pitcher who qualified for this honor was Fred Ianuzzi. Coming off a no hitter against The Forresters, the bashful southpaw aced the Firemen 3-0. Versus the Firemen, Gotti scored first, in the fourth inning against Bill Sheehan to wrap up game one. In game two, the Firemen rallied past the Gotti Nine by A sore of 11-3. The Firemen brought out the lumber via monsieurs McGuire, Miller, Reifenberger and Dinzer.

Game three was won by the Gotti Nine and placed them in a direct line to the Royals. A grand collision was coming. With the championship on the line, Fred Ianuzzi toed the rubber carrying forward a sting of 28 consecutive shutout innings! If MVP awards were given, Fred would certainly lead the voting.

In the Community playoffs, the Orioles edged Wanaque. Pat Dorme's finely tuned pitching clinched the first game. Game two went to Wanaque's by an 8 to 3 margin

> **Game Three was won by the Gotti Nine and placed them In a direct line to the Royals. A grand collision was coming...**

CHAMPIONSHIP
Royals vs Gotti Nine

52

The sports reporter from the Standard Star led off his column to indicate Lady Luck was in the Royal corner in the first game of a best-of-four for the city title.

Ty Cobb once said "Luck is the residue of design" This underscored the Royal's penchant for winning. They took every advantage of an opponents" miscues.

With a City Park attendance estimated at 300 to 400 spectators on hand to see the matchup, the Gotti 9 held a one run lead going into the final frame.

In fact, they needed just one more out to pull a major upset. Royal manager Will Richardson recalled opposing pitcher Lefty Ianuzzi had a sore knee from the series with the Firemen, a week prior.

It was this close attention to detail the Royals would use. With two out, they brilliantly utilized the squeeze play catching Lefty off guard. Barely fielding the bunt, Ianuzzi threw the ball into right field.

The Royals win. But it wasn't over yet. Game Two was won by the irrepressible Ianuzzi, 3 to 0.

But the Royals buried Gotti in the finale, 13 to 9, with about 300 attendees witnessing a vintage Bob Simmons one hitter, marred by a lone single from Ray Budetti.

There was some controversey that year. Home plate umpire Nello Amori -- despite protestations from Gotti -- called the final game due to darkness after five innings.

Sports beat writer Pat McGowan wrote that Stroman and Richardson of the champion Royals "have no peer at their position" in either softball or basketball."

The Royals were triumphant despite close calls. They could now place their championship status side by side with their other trophies and call their team "dynasty."

If there were any question that they had got a break from Nello Amori that year, they would disprove doubters next season...

1953

Catching Legends of Fast-Pitch Play · 53

Wes Westrum was the catcher for the New York Giants from 1947 to 1957. His baseball skills were on the defensive side, though he had a knack for hitting home runs in key situations. In 1950, he set a National League record -- a .999 fielding percentage.

His fielding (one error in 680 chances) was extraordinary. In 1954's World Series he hit .273 with three runs batted in as he faced off against the American League's best defensive catcher Jim Hegan of the Indians.

His work with the Giants 1951 staff of Maglie, Jansen and Hearn helped the Giants catch the Dodgers during their great comeback. Tough, gritty and a keen observer, Westrum managed the Mets in 1966 to 67. As a catcher, Westrum typified the model for softball players too; that is, handle pitchers, have knowledge of the opponents hitters, and have strong arm to cut down potential base stealers.

The Twilight League had its share of good defensive catchers. Though the softball game played in the 1950s was pitcher centric, catchers had to be tough. The equipment was barely protective. Nicks and bruises came with the turf. It is easy to see why.

The equipment consisted of a flimsy catcher's mask held together with a Band-Aid, one piece of thin wire as frame, an occasional chest protector and - if available - a wafer-thin shard of cloth with sponge-like filling. Wearing a protective cup was entirely up to the user. What size and strength they utilized was also a matter of choice. For those who got hit in the family jewels, the pain had an intensity of cross between a kidney stone and a shotgun wound.

Here are some catchers who led the league in excellence:

Pint Murray & Earl Williams: (Royals) Both were meticulous in handling pitchers, which meant Bob Simmons and Bill Marino most of the time. Each were contact hitters, limited their strikeouts and exhibited smart baseball sense.

George Gallo: (Popeye 9) A consistent line drive hitter, very competitive, accurate thrower, choked up on bat to spray ball anywhere on the field. Tended to back up on hits to first base - a hustler

Horace Lybrand (Tectape) A lefty swinger, very powerful, could hit it out of the park, good defensive catcher too.

Don Zack (Feeney Park)- also hit for power, rocket arm, understood hitting and delivered in the clutch

Sal Oliverios (Warrens) underrated backstop---athletic, worked hard for every hit, very good defensive catcher.

COLD WAR
Great Times and All Things Pax Americana

53

The year 1953 marked the passing of Joseph Stalin. For America, it represented the removal of a psychological weight, the ponderous responsibility of leading the free world against tyranny and communism. For the next few decades, the U.S. would follow the political and economic theories of George Keenan, Secretary of State under Eisenhower, to reinforce the policy of containment- a duplicitous game of chess involving the whole world. This required astute management in counterbalancing U.S. and Soviet power—a high stakes game which the U.S. would eventually win. Although there was a cold war to wage, America felt good. This was the Pax Americana, the period to look ahead, develop new products, big cars, smoke cigarettes, construct new housing, celebrate the family, and play.

No Rock-N-Roll, Just Listening Booths

The post war babies hadn't made their musical mark yet. Vocalists Frankie Laine, Jo Stafford, Eddie Fisher...even Mantovani cracked the Top-Forty list in 1953. Movies were non controversial. The Robe and Shane topped the box-office charts. The U.S. was in relax mode. No rock, no roll -- not yet. New Rochelle had three music shops. One, A&D Music was on North Avenue near Camera Craft. It offered music labels like Decca, Victor and Mercury and 45s at 69 cents each. In their ads, "all categories" of music are said to be available: jazz, pop, classical, and hillbilly. Hillbilly? Apparently "country" was a foreign term in "these there parts."

Still, Frank's Music Shop on Huguenot Street would sell vinyl, but if you wanted he'd group your purchases together, and when you reached 10, you'd receive one free. Another attraction for Frank's was his glass-windowed listening booths where customers could "try out" a record before purchase.

New Rochelle's
Talk of the Town

1953

Fort Slocum:
PT Boats, Nike Missles and Baseball

New Rochelle was rocked by the announcement that the federal government was closing down Fort Slocum. Mayor Stanley W. Church filed a protest with Westchester's congressional group citing economic ramifications. Little did Church know how this would be a political football all the way to the current year. The military post was abandoned by the Army in 1948. The island had been in use by the military since the Civil War, serving as a hospital for wounded Union troops. In World War II, it served as a site for PT Boat construction. And in the mid-1950s, it would serve as Nike Missile base, protecting against the possibility of a Soviet strike.

In the 1990s, Donald Trump and developers would propose a housing development aimed at attracting Hong Kong residents looking for a new island as Britain exited and a Chinese government took the reins. Like many others, before and since, development was blocked. The island today sits like a lost colony in the Long Island Sound. However, during the early 1950s, Fort Slocum had remained an integral part of the city and had its own Twilight League ball club, schools, homes, churches and a hotel.

KEEPING ENTERTAINED

In 53', The Elmsford Drive-In showed "Beast from 50,000 Fathoms." Live entertainment flourished. The Empire Club on North Avenue had a piano bar as well as a dinner special of steak dinner for $1.50. Tompkins on Main St. in New Rochelle had music nightly, featuring the Tony Oliver Trio and weekend dancing. Terrace Lounge's Carolyn Wood sang nightly and headed a "Hawaiian" floor show.

New Rochelle's
Talk of the Town

1953

Elizabeth II

June brought with it the magnificent spectacle of Britain's coronation of its new queen, Elizabeth II, with all the pageantry and elegance expected in a once-in-a-lifetime event. Television networks raced to be the first broadcaster of the mega event. As cascades of voices uttered "God Save the Queen," echoing across the regent landscape as millions watched the ceremony on television. As her son Charles impatiently looked on, twenty-seven-year-old Elizabeth was noticeably worn down by the goings on but seemed to settle down when her purple and gold coach took her and her entourage to Old London Town.

Frisch Speaks

In White Plains, keynote speaker and Hall of Famer Frankie Frisch shared the dais with announcer Don Dunphy and the defensive lineman Andy Robustelli of the Los Angeles Rams.

The occasion was the Westchester Sports Forum. Dunphy who announced more heavyweight fights than any announcer correctly predicted Marciano's reign as champ for about 4-5 more years. Marciano retired in 1956.

MEMORIAL DEDICATION

On Memorial Day, New Rochelle officials gathered together to dedicate a new elementary school, George M, Davis. with invocations by Rabbi Freille, Monsignor Fitzgerald, Reverend Styles, and Mayor Stanley Church.

TALNER'S JEWELERS

In June 1953, one of New Rochelle's recognizable retailers opened its doors.It was the grand opening of Talner's Jewelers, which today is still thriving and heading for its 60th birthday.

New Rochelle's
Talk of the Town

1953

Those Dangerous Trolley Cars!

On the local scene, it was noted that a fixture at Main and Division streets for 30 years, "Big John" Haley was retiring from the New Rochelle Police force after manning that post since 1922. From that position, cars and truckers would invariably ask for directions. Haley recalled a situation where he almost lost it all…a trolley car ran the light, striking him. He was lucky to just have injured a knee. What changed the tempo of Main Street was it becoming one way and the increase in the speed limit. Haley said Main Street, prior to those changes, had been a more "serene" thoroughfare.

Faces and Places

In New Rochelle, the NR Federal Savings and Loan on North Avenue was showing an exhibit of antique toy banks. At the high school, future Dobie Gillis and Gilligan's Island star, Bob Denver, was missed by friends who lamented his recent move to Texas. Over at Iona College, Richie Guerin was pouring in an average of 19 points per game on the basketball court. Downtown, Arnold Constable and Bloomingdale's decorated front windows with the latest styles, and on Huguenot Street, a city worker swept debris with his garbage can on wheels.

REMEMBERING NEW ROCHELLE'S FIELD ENFORCER

He was as fine a gentleman as you would ever meet. Louis Grossi was night "Rec" director and part of his job was to make sure that while softball games were being played at Columbus Field there was no interference by dogs, kids or anyone who might wander onto the baseball area. No one took their job as seriously. In his sixties, Mr. Grossi was a rabid Notre Dame fan full of stories about the Irish. Despite his age, some fans recall his running at full speed like a Notre Dame linebacker to catch a youthful trespasser cutting across center field to take a short cut to Feeney Park or the Boys Club also located there.

Rivalries Renewed
The Bonnies Best the Knights in Early Play

As the calendar hit April and the temperature touched 60, Mike Cesario and several boys took out their baseball mitts and headed to Jefferson School to hit ground balls and have a catch. Praise the Lord -- it was springtime and the sound of bats and balls was around the bend.

Fans looked forward to the confrontation between the Trotters and Bonefro

On Fourth Street, John Claps answered his phone "Union !" at Union Auto Repair. Recreation Commissioner Fred Todora had been trying to reach Popeye Claps to let him know, the Department had approved the name change of his team (the Orioles) to the "Popeye Nine." New uniform shirts had to be ordered for the season with a small logo of "Popeye" stitched on.

In the first meaningful game of the budding season, an unbeaten Bonefro Club registered its third victory by upending the Knights, 9 to 5. Bert Terranova had a 3 for 3 night for the Bonnies. Their next game was against the undefeated Trotters who had now changed their name from the Royals. As usual, there were three leagues under the management of the Recreation Commission: the Senior, Industrial and Community leagues. In other action, City Park rose up to throttle Washingon AC, 9 to 4, behind the pitching of Chuck Columbo.

Fans looked forward to the confrontation between the Trotters and Bonefro. Ever since the Rec Department placed these talent-laden teams in the Senior League, devotees of the game couldn't wait for the fireworks. The result of the first showdown was favorable for the Bonnies as hard throwing Joe Connelly kept the Trotters in check for a surprisingly easy win.

To sum up, if handicappers put up odds at the start of the season, Bonefro Club would be even with the Trotters to take the Senior League, the Police would take the Industrial and the Popeye Nine - the Community.

On the same day, the Trotters rallied to tie the Curlers 8 to 8 in Senior League activity, catcher E. Williams of the Trotters went 3 for 3 and left the Curlers near the top of the standings with the Bonnies.

53

New Rochelle Recreation Department Supervisor Fred Todora Announces Early Twilight League Standings

Senior Division

1	Bonefro Club	4-0
2	Trotters	3-1
3	Echo Bay	3-2
4	Curlers	3-2
5	City Park	3-2
6	Red Eye	2-3
7	Washington AC	2-3
8	Knights	1-4
9	Jesters	0-5

Industrial Division

1	Tectape	5-0
2	Police	3-2
3	Empire	3-1
4	Firemen	3-2
5	Talco	3-2
6	Teevees	3-2
7	Snapples	2-3
8	554 Club	2-3
9	Darts	0-4
10	TMC	0-5

Community Division

1	Robins	4-0
2	Popeye Nine	3-1
3	Outlaws	2-3
4	American Legion	1-3
5	Warrens	1-3
6	Jaycees	0-5

Bonnies Remain Unbeaten
Tectape Sticks to Its Game Plan

The immediate game drawing the most attention was the Popeye vs Robins contest. Due to wet grounds, all other games were cancelled except Columbus Field which absorbed water very well. As usual, scorekeeper Fred D'piano obtained the lineups from each team manager prior to start of the game.

After Cookie Norberto cracked a line drive homer which cleared the right field fence and landed in Mr. Esposito's tomato garden gave the Robins a 1 to 0 lead, the Popeyes countered with two runs in the bottom of the inning putting together scores resulting from a walk to leadoff man Tony Giordano and rbi's from Mike Macri and Charlie Ariginello. With Rocco Orsini having a perfect 3 for 3 night and Pat Dorme twirling a four hitter, the Popeye 9 handled the Redbirds fairly easily, 10 to 4. Both teams, comprised mostly of recently graduated high schoolers represented up and coming talent in the sport.

The Bonnies continued unbeaten with a 9 to 3 triumph over Echo Bay. Joe Connelly again starred in the win, allowing only six hits while nabbing two base hits himself. Over at Jefferson, the City Park clobbered a completely outclassed Jesters, 20 to 4.

Norberto cracked a line drive homer which cleared the right field fence

Not so serene was the jockeying for position in the softball leagues. In the Industrial League, Team 554 nipped Snapple, 8 to 7, on a game winning hit by 554 pitcher Al Strasser. Also in the Industrial League, the Police toppled Empire Cell, 9 to 7, to gain a tie with Tectape.

They scored eight times in the top of the first inning as righhander Jerry Uzzillo held on for the victory. The Robins had trumped the Warrens in the Community League 5 to 4 to pull ahead of the Popeyes by a full game in the standings. Momentum was shifting for Tectape as they edged the Police 6 to 4 in a playoff game for the first round.

Paul Kipp hit a three run homer in the first inning which was the key to the Tectape win. Danny Brandon closed out the last three innings for Tectape and got the win.

Bonnies "On a Rampage"
The Knights became Bonefro's 14th victim

After being upset by the Knights, the Trotters faced Echo Bay in a crucial match. The pressure fell on Bill Marino to help get the win.....and that he did - tossing a sparkling one hitter. The final score: Trotters 2, Echo Bay 1. Willie Archer provided the offense for the Trotters. The red hot Bonefro Club captured their 11th-straight win paced by timely hits from Iarocci, Funicello and Connelly in crunching the Forresters, 8 to 3. At this point, the Bonnies were favorites to take the title. The only question was about their pitching.

Their lineup was certainly a formidable one.

Bonefro celebrated. They notched their 12th consecutive win backed by Len Piedmont's six hitter against Washington A.C. The game was a definitive rout, 17 to 0. Iarocci, DiBuono & Esposito, sounding like an Italian law firm, provided the muscle. Echo Bay socked Red Eye, 8 to 1,

behind Jack Meehan's roundtripper.

If Bonefro was putting the pressure on the them, the second place Trotters did not show it. Al Flowers and Horace Lybrand whacked homers in support of Bill Marino as they stopped the Washington AC. There was no problem for Bonefro as they next annihilated Red Eye, 21 to 0. That same evening, the Knights beat Echo Bay, 10 to 3—two games with football-like scores.

The Knights became Bonefro's 14th victim with a 10 to 3 drubbing at City Park. Joe Connelly's blazing fastball kept the Knights at bay. In other games, Don Summo of the Outlaws clouted a homer to defeat the Warrens.

A Turning Point: The game everyone anticipated had arrived on Thursday night July 2nd—an estimated 400 fans crowded into City Park to see a Connelly-versus-Marino matchup. Bonefro Club vs the Trotters.

The Bonnie Lineup

```
1b-Iarocci
2b-Burigo
ss-DiBuono
3b-Esposito
lf-Funicello
cf-Mandarano
rf-Terranova
c- Connelly
p -Piedmont
```

End of a Streak
The Bonnies had Swept 16 Straight

53

Will Richardson broke the ice with an RBI single to right, resulting in catcher Earl Williams scoring. Vic Gibson's blast off of Connelly was the clincher. Pitcher Marino delivered in the clutch again. For the Trotters it was a significant win but for Bonefro the sting of a loss would last long after the game. If this book was done as a movie, we'd hear in the background something like the 1953 jukebox hit Crying in the Chapel. The good news for the Bonnies was that they were still in first place. For the Trotters, the road back was uphill. On July 1st, they were in fourth place in the senior division.

Meanwhile, the Curlers slowly moved closer into second place in the senior circuit by beating Echo Bay, 4 to 0. The Trotters suffered another loss this time to the Forresters. Even though they outhit the Forresters , 10-6, the final score had the Forresters firmly ahead, 6 to 3.

Prospects for the Trotters grew dimmer in terms of repeating as champs. Another softball franchise, Tectape also lost a close one as they bowed to Empire, 6 to 5. Bob Green had three hits for Empire. The Popeye

Nine solidified their hold on first place in the Community League by rounding up the Outlaws, 9 to 5. The Outlaws took a 4-0 lead, but Popeyes answered with nine scoring runs. Tony Giordano had a 3 for 3 day, and Pat Dorme picked up the win.

All summer long, the Bonnies ran up impressive wins even managing to win 16 straight but in the first playoff game against the Curlers fell, 3 to 2, in a major upset. Also at Moore Field, the Trotters wound up on top, 4 to 1, over the Forresters.

As playoffs continued, Bonefro took advantage of the Curlers only having eight players and evened up the series, 1-1. Ken Kasara held the Bonnies to three hits in a gallant effort. Earl Williams - 4 for 4 - boosted the Trotters. A two hitter from Dan Brandon of Tectape enabled the Tapes to finish the season at 17-3 with Empire ending its season at a very successful 18-4. Dick Forst of Empire was effective in holding the Tapes to six hits.

The Playoffs Began, the Bonnies Tumbled

Playoffs

Popeye standouts were "Pigeon" Ariganello and Pat Dorme

Momentum built on the side of the Trotters as they met the Bonefro Club in Game One of the Industrial/Senior League playoff. Throughout, Bonefro displayed a porous defense, which combined with Marino's tight pitching, allowed the Trotters to claim victory. Three Bonefro throws to first base went errant allowing the Trotters to score a run. The Bonnies scored on a wild pitch by Marino. Final: Trotters 2, Bonefro 1

With their backs to the wall, the Bonnies met the Trotters at Moore Field (Isaac Young) to determine the championship in the Senior League. The Trotters didn't have their best year. And the Bonnies felt it was their year of destiny.

One armed Bill Marino would be the MVP of the playoffs, if the award existed. Used to fighting uphill battles, the husky

The Bonnies Had Their Backs to the Wall

righthander fired a three hitter to eliminate the Bonnies. Horace

The Popeyes took charge early to vanquish the new challenger

Lybrand hit another homer to pace the Trotters.

In other playoff action, the Popeye Nine, with Pat Dorme hurling a two hitter, edged the Robins, 2 to 1, in Game One of the Community League Playoffs. Dorme had pitched brilliantly the previous night but appeared sharp in the win over the Robins. Only a single from Gate D'Attilo and a double by John DeMasi kept Dorme from a no-hitter. The hitting standouts for Popeye were Joe Carpanzano, "Pigeon" Ariganello, and captain Tony Giordano.In Game Two, the Popeyes took charge early to vanquish the new challenger, the Robins, 11 to 2 . Joe Grossi, the first baseman for the Popeyes homered and continued his torrid pace.

Trotters
Simmons Silences the Bats

The Trotters' attention now zeroed in on Tectape, their perennial nemesis. Bobby Simmons was sharp in shutting down Tectape's offense with only one hit. Al Flowers and Will Richardson carried the Trotter's by each smacking a homer. Final: Trotters 8, Tectape 0. Game Two of the series saw Bill Marino at his best limiting Tectape to two hits.

With one out in the bottom of the first inning, Massey the Tectape pitcher walked catcher Earl Williams. A sacrifice fly got Williams to second, and he scored when Richardson lined a single to right giving the Trotters all they would need. Final: Trotters 4, Tectape 0.

It was an incredible year of turnarounds. The Trotters (aka Royals) were lackluster most of the year but stopped two streaky teams in the playoffs—Bonefro and Tectape. They were "Toast of the Town" to borrow a phrase from Ed Sullivan. And the town, New Rochelle, toasted their accomplishment.

1954

Local Views

Talk of the Town in New Rochelle

Cross County

April 1954 saw the opening of the first open-air shopping center in New York at Cross County Plaza in Yonkers, the largest retail development ever for Westchester County. It also became widely known from frequent visits made by Allen Funt, who liked to use the venue as a backdrop for his Candid Camera show.

The shopping center beckoned visitors from the Tri-State Area to walk along its "elegant" promenade.

Celebrity visitors appearing the first week were Carl Reiner, Martha Raye, Jackie Cooper, Henny Youngman, and the cast of WWOR's The McCanns.

Above the Sound

A little known incident in local history, a near catastrophe, took place in the airspace above the New Rochelle-Larchmont border on June 10, 1953. A U.S. Air Force jet that lost its tail fin over the city of Yonkers, tried to stay airborne and veered east at highspeed. The pilot narrowly missed crashing into downtown New Rochelle. As the plane burst aflame, Lt. Dan O'Connell bailed out at 1,000 feet into the waters of the Sound where a boater picked him up and raced him to New Rochelle Hospital.

ROCKY MARCIANO GOES THE DISTANCE IN TITLE DEFENSE

In June 1954, an unbeaten Rocky Marciano was scheduled to take on a tough veteran in Ezzard Charles. The challenger was more physically imposing than Marciano. Taller than Marciano and having a reach advantage, Charles was still an underdog. In a brutal bloody match, Marciano won by a decision at the close of Round 15. A fiery Marciano pummelled Charles in the last few rounds, ensuring victory. Though he lost the bout, Charles was the sole fighter to go the distance against Marciano.

IONA PITCHER GOES PRO

Local Sports Hero Valentinetti Takes on New York Yanks

Vito Valentinetti was the first Iona College grad to make the major leagues. The journeyman hurler pitched for several teams including the White Sox. On the 20th of June 1954, the Chisox were playing a doubleheader with the Yankees in Chicago. Vito was called on to pitch the ninth inning with his team trailing 10 to 6. Appearing in his first major league game was like stepping into a dream.

```
'Yankees'
Rizzuto   SS
Noren     LF
Mantle    CF
Berra     C
Bauer     RF
Skowron   1B
McDougal  3B
Coleman   2B
Reynolds  P
```

The 6 foot 1 inch righty took the ball, surveyed the outfield and began warming up. His pitches had good velocity but didn't quite have that "hop" or deft movement. He quickly looked around to reassure himself he was truly on the mound at Comiskey Park.

```
'White Sox'
Carresquel  SS
Fox         2B
Minoso      LF
Fain        1B
Kell        3B
Savatski    C
Rivera      RF
Groth       CF
Pierce      P
```

Umpire Bill Sommers made a motion to begin play. Here he was facing the vaunted Yankees in all their glory. What a way to break into the majors!

In the ninth inning, the first Yankee batter Vito Valentinetti faced was Johnny Sain. He popped out to second baseman Nellie Fox. The next batter, Phil Rizzuto drew a walk. Willie Miranda stepped in as pinch runner for Rizzuto. Noren doubled the first pitch to right field with Miranda going to third. Mantle walked. Berra then unloaded on a 2-2 pitch to left center for a three bagger. Next, Leja ran for exhausted Berra. And Gene Woodling singled, followed by a Joe Collins homer. Bobby Brown fanned and a Coleman hit flew "out."

Thus completed Valentinetti's opening game which Yanks won 16 to 6. It wasn't very encouraging, but he had officially made it to the big time. And after all, this was the 1954 Yankees...

Other Iona College players eventually followed Valentinetti to the majors : Dennis Leonard, and Mike Bertotti.

(The most recent Gael gone pro is Jason Motte who plays for the St. Louis Cardinals.)

Many play baseball but only a few are fortunate to make it to that level. In 1953, there were only 16 major league clubs, compared to 30 today so making the cut was far less likely for second tier talent.

Twilight Leaguers that made the minors in the 1950s were Sil Burigo, Nick Bombace, Joe Carpanzano , Bruno Terilli, and Al Ryder.

Double Feature: It Came from Home Plate

Foul Balls

54

Softballs purchased at Allen's Sports Shop cost an expensive $1.25 in 1954, and were therefore carefully conserved and marshaled by umpire crews.

Amazingly, balls knocked or popped onto Seventh Street at Columbus Field were seldom "stolen" by neighborhood kids and were typically returned to the umpire, as if by some unwritten rule. Not only were the majority of balls returned, but kids would search them out in bushes and even in municipal sewer tunnels.

Fouls were mostly routine. But strange occurrences did happen. New Rochelle's City Park typically saw more pedestrians pegged than other fields. D'Onofrio Field featured all sorts of environmental hazards to contend with when recovering fouls. Balls might land in the nearby dog kennel or in a thicket of overgrown vegetation on the left side of the field.

A close watch of softball supply was important to play. An objective was to keep the less tarnished baseballs for the late innings as twilight time approached. With no stadium lights, it was easier for a batter to see a cleaner ball. Scuffed balls might prove an almost invisible and dangerous projectile, post twilight.

WHO DARED DENT MY DESOTO?

At one game at City Park involving the Royals, a man parked his shiny 1953 DeSoto in an isolated spot, but one easily within range of left field's foul zone. A batter hit a foul ball that put a dent in the hood. The irate owner then held up the start of the next inning, asking the home plate umpire who he should contact about repairing his car. Not getting an answer, the man drove off in his DeSoto. In 1954, there were no assurances that anyone actually had insurance.

Keeping attuned to local happenings

Pitching Duel and a Future Yankee

It wasn't Twilight League Softball, but it was one of the most memorable moments in local sports that year. Two ace pitchers that led in no-hitters in high-school play were slated for a showdown.

Stepinac's Tony Amendola was up against Terry Reilly of Blessed Sacrament. The much-anticipated cross-county rivalry saw Stepinac manage a 4 to 0 romp.

Three of Stepinac's 13 hits came from none other Jim DePalo. This same slugger would make it all the way to the major leagues where he would play for the New York Yanks.

Your Hit Parade

In television programming, every Saturday night was "live" in 1954.

Among these were some of the most memorable shows in TV history. On the tube one primetime was "The Martha Raye Show" featuring an appearance by middleweight boxing champ Rocky Graziano.

Viewers were also treated to comedy of Herb Shriner and Amos & Andy. Wrestling also took to the airwaves, and one of the most popular shows was Your Hit Parade.

Radio listeners tuned into the Johnny Mercer Show on WCBS, Gangbusters on WABC, Family Theatre on WWOR, and Dance Party on WABC

SUMMERING IN NEW ROCHELLE

Major league pitcher Larry Jansen of the New York Giants, along with his wife and seven children, made friends with local fans in 1954 when they chose to summer in New Rochelle. The Jansens joined the New Rochelle Yacht Club and themselves became fans of the Sound Shore .

FUNNY PAPERS

Comic strips in newspapers became an increasingly important feature of American culture. Poking fun at each other and at our institutions was a popular theme in 1954. The most-read strips were Bringing Up Father, Mandrake the Magician, Donald Duck, Myrtle, and I Love Lucy

MEET THE UMPIRES

These folks, ranging in age from 30s to 50s, were just as colorful as any of the players during the Twilight Era. Paid by the recreation department, they received little formal training and relied on life experiences and seat-of-the-pants common sense to govern games. Frequently, especially for big games, players showed great interest in who was umpiring. Each ump had a different strike zone which proved an important factor in determining a contest's winner.

At each game, there were usually two umps – one behind the catcher and one to man the bases. If only one was available, he would "call" balls and strikes from behind the pitcher's mound. Playoffs would usually have a third umpire to better cover the field.

Amiable, each also had a boiling point. This was before the era of inflated chest protectors. But if you irked them by challenging a call, you might expect some hot air.

Meet the umps:

Sidney Lee: probably had the longest tenure of all the umps despite attempts by some players to pay for weekly checkups at the optometrist. Sid was serious and seldom broke a smile. He kept games orderly and always fair.

George Battle: seemingly always involved in the big games, he would not allow any discussion of his always correct decisions. If you argued with him, he'd walk away. "The less said, the better the result" was his philosophy.

Ed DiNapoli: a magnet for disputes, this mild-mannered cigar smoker (unlike the two men above) actually enjoyed banter from players.

Sal Sclafani: another cigar enthusiast, Sal was all business, not tolerant of arguments, and sought to move the game along. He was also a player in years he did not umpire.

Nello Amori: always ready to explain decisions, if necessary, he ran a smooth game and didn't mind chatter with players who universally respected him.

Sonny Funicello: pleasant umpire who wasn't afraid of confrontations, he was one of the most likeable of all men in blue.

Jerry Hempfield: a younger ump, he kept a distance from players, Decisions were definitive and he detested any dissent over his calls.

Joe Piedmont: among the "most experienced" umpires, Joe called games with effortless ease. He was tough on players who challenged him, but liked to hear a good joke. He knew when to get serious. He also survived a lightning strike on the field.

Pete Accocella: Like George Battle, he always kept his cool and was a real gentleman. He was an efficient ump and kept game moving quickly.

Ernie Motta: fiery and emotional, if challenged. He could not be matched vocally in disputes.

Robert Walker: easy going, he gave explanations for decisions. Certainly, he was among the most pleasant umps.

Al Barilari: always efficient and very distant. He didn't care for confrontation.

Pint Murray: a prior player for the Royals, he was considerate of both sides of an argument and was very professional.

Lou Carideo: affable, talkative and astute. Keen to explain ground rules, he made good judgments.

Seely Burigo: fair and reasonable, easy going, and knowledgeable.

Tectape: An Industrial Powerhouse
Perri Expected Great Things from Players

A classic rivalry of 1950s Twilight League play was between two storied New Rochelle softball clubs -- the reigning champs -- the Royals and an upstart challenger known as Tectape.

The Tectapers were the perennial champs of the so-called Industrial League, a division of clubs sponsored by local companies for their employees.

About a third of the Twilight Leagues 20 clubs belonged to the Industrial Division.

The Tectapers were the most prominent, representing the Tuck Tape company located near the waterfront in the East End of the city, off of Boston Post Road. Tectape clinched the most Industrial League titles for the decade.

Businesses sponsoring sports teams was still a new idea in the 1950s. And the thriving success of New Rochelle's fast-pitch softball leagues, to some degree, was possible only because local factories were thriving and therefore willing to assume the modest costs of sponsoring teams.

Local businesses like Tuck Tape Industries saw sports sponsorship as a way to offer factory employees a vigorous exercise regimen that was better than modern health club memberships. It was meant to be recreational. It also became the foundation of friendships and an inspiration for both teamwork and competitiveness.

One person who epitomized the spirit of this effort was Techtape General Manager Mario Perri, who coached both the company softball club and its basketball team.

Committed to winning, Perri brought almost a religious zeal to his brand of coaching, expecting great things from players and usually getting it. Perri molded a disciplined team, a fact demonstrated by Techtape's impressive win record. Tectape typically took the title in the industrial division. And in 1954, this seemed likely again thanks to a quick throwing lanky right-hander, Danny Brandon who was in top form.

Brandon showed his prowess early in the 1954 Season, helping his team extinguish the New Rochelle Fire Department with a final score of 6 to 4. Perri's Tectapers were on an early roll, but it remained to be seen if they were up to the job of finally besting their nemesis, the Royals.

Playing for the Company
Second-ranked Splicers cut into Tectape's Comfort Zone

54

Another Industrial League team, the Splicers would tie the firemen in their season opener. The game was notable for a Fire Department round tripper by Blessed Sacrament graduate Larry Hennessey who the next year would begin his professional career as an NBA player, joining the Philadelphia Warriors for two seasons before being traded to Syracuse Nationals.

New Rochelle's Fort Slocum club kicked off its Industrial League opener by nipping Technical Material Corp.'s team (TMC), 7 to 6.

In a second showdown , the Splicers continued on a winning note with six runs in the second inning, beating TMC with a final of 7 to 5. This win put the Splicers on strong footing, placing the team on an eventual collision course with Tectape for the division title.

West New Rochelle Rivals

In the Community League, the division with the youngest talent, action commenced in earnest with the Warrens edging the Scorpions, 6 to 5.

Next, the Washington AC upended the Carl's, 9 to 1. The following week Skip Gamble led the Warrens with three hits while pitcher Ernie Flowers registered his second win.

In a key early matchup, the Popeye Nine held off a rally by the Warrens, winning 11 to 9. The Ariginello brothers, Sal and Anthony "Pigeon," provided the offensive energy for the Popeye Nine, offering a speed advantage over their West New Rochelle rivals.

In their next outing, Jimmy Sabia of the Popeye's smacked two doubles to spark a victory over the Scorpions, 8 to 4.

Even so, the Community Division's Bonefro Club looked like a team to beat when they crushed the Knights, 6 to 0. Pitcher Len Piedmont allowed no hits .

The Bonnies, this season, were stacked with dangerous players. These included pitching ace Vin Connelly , Pete Gillespie, slugger "Tut" Mandarano , Al Ryder, and 'Iceman' Iarocci.

The Royals, sticking with their winning formula, curbed the Curlers in their opener. Bobby Simmons notched his first win. Next, Ianuzzi handcuffed a new entry in the league, the Jeeps to lead the Gotti Nine to victory.

Pitching Duel
Bonnies' Connelly vs. Royals' McClendon

54

There were strange happenings in a game between TMC and GRC. A heated dispute developed on a close play at second base. TMC refused to take the field. With no other choice, the umpires called the game a forfeit.

"Warneke" Caizzo, manager of the Orchids took his team to Columbus Field to take on the contending Warrens. Gabe Carino of the Orchids faced off against Ernie Flowers. Carino pitched very well allowing only two hits but a leaky defense allowed 7 runs to score. Result: Warrens 7, Orchids 3.

In other contests, Washington AC's Bob Fay helped himself to three hits - as Washington defeated the Scorpions. The City Park Jeeps crushed the Forrestors, 16 to 6, with Lefty Immediato stroking three hits. Securing their first win, the Firemen celebrated long into the night.

Next was a classic head-to-head match. One of the memorable games of 1954 was a confrontation between Vin Connelly (Bonnies) and Norm McClendon (Royals), two of the area's best softball pitchers. McClendon started for the Royals. Connelly toed the mark for Bonefro Club.

The Royals struck first going up 2 to 0 on Earl Williams key hit to drive in Will Richardson. Nipping away at this lead, the Bonnies scored one run in the bottom of the third, fifth and sixth innings and upset the Royals, 3 to 2. Joe Rainieri went two- -for-three and scored twice.

As the weather warmed up, batting averages also went up.

Some notable slugfests followed contests. The hard hitting Curlers scored three in the second, paced by Joe Santoro connecting for a four bagger to down the Knights, 7 to 4.

A seesaw contest at City Park saw the Jeeps outlast the Coral Reefs, 11 to 10.

Bonefro Club continued its winning ways with an 11 to 6 blowout of Bowl-o-Bar. John Mandarano (3 for 4) and first baseman Meehan provided key swings.

Horace Lybrand socked a homer to enable Tectape to topple GBC, 5 to 3.

Pat Dorme's steady pitching arm helped Popeye Nine to stomp the Warrens, 9 to 1.

Techtapers, Royals and Popeye Niners
Mismatches Marked by a Bonanza of Blowouts

In the Industrial League, Tectape and the Splicers were ranked first and second, respectively. The Splicers romped over Empire Cell, 11 to 3. Tapers edged Fort Slocum, 6 to 5. Sal Sclafani got a win for unbeaten Tectape and also drove in the deciding Ken Kruger went 3 for 4 to lead Tectape.

Mario Perri, coach of the Tectapers had his team on top in the Industrial League - clearly "the class" of that division. They squashed the Snapples 23 to 3, while Bonefro Club rolled over Coral Reef, 8 to 1.

Clearly, this time period saw an imbalance in the quality of the teams that faced off, as box-score blowouts bloomed.

Matching teams to the right level of competition was something league planners and schedule makers would take a hard look at after some infamous 1954 mismatches.

Bonefro Club clinched at a tie for the first round final with Len Piedmont pitching his second no hitter of the month by whitewashing the Jeeps, 6 to 0.

Tom Napolitano's three hits, along with Pete Gillespie's dual doubles, paced the Bonnies.

When the Knights beat the Royals - 6 to 3 - on leftfielder Goldman's two hits and Rodham's double, some fans questioned the Royal's dominance.

That would remain to be seen. During the same night, the

```
        With a third of games played,
            the top teams were:

SENIOR        INDUSTRIAL      COMMUNITY
1.Bonefro     Tectape         Washington AC
2.Gotti 9     Firemen         Popeye Nine
3.Royals      Splicers        Warrens
4.Curlers     Empire Cell     Orchids
```

Orchids upset Washington AC, 7 to 3, with Gabe Carino as the winning pitcher.

The team with the distinction of scoring the most runs that season were the Firemen who tallied 13 runs in the top of the first inning. The final tally Firemen 27, Griers Reproducer Corp, 4. Of the 33 hits gathered by the Firemen, a number came from from Seely Burigo and Larry Hennessey.

Techtape vs. Popeye Nine

Popeyes Take on an Industrial Giant in Championship Race

54

Just before the playoffs were to start, fans were wondering if this was the year some team would find a way to beat the Royals. Bonefro Club quickly answered the question. The Bonnies crushed the Royals, 5 to 1.

Tut Mandarano of the Bonnies, batting fifth in the lineup, smashed 3 hits to lead the way. For the first time in quite a while, the Royals were stopped stone cold.

To get to the championship series, the Popeyes had to win two of three games against the Orchids. In Game One, the Orchids defeated the "Niners," 3 to 2. Game Two was a tight seesaw affair with the Orchids trying to pull a major upset. They had the Popeyes down 6 to 2 after three frames. To comprehend the intensity of this local rivalry, one must realize that Popeye's candy store was located at Fifth Street and Warneke, manager of the Orchids, lived about three houses away. So the winner won hyperlocal "bragging rights".

The Popeye's comeback began with Jim Sabia's soft single to right center. Mickey Circelli doubled and Sabia toed home plate. Slowly, the Popeyes rebounded and ultimately took the lead, ending the game 7 to 6.

Now it was on to Game Three. The Popeyes came up with six runs in the first inning keyed by Mickey Circelli's double. The Orchids, however, refused to quit. Ron Semenza's hits produced two runs for the Orchids and Cookie Norberto landed a third run as Popeye pitcher Pat Dorme held tough for the win. It marked the last game of the West New Rochelle rivalry.

Following their last minute heroics to defeat the Orchids, the Popeye Niners engaged powerful Tectape in a test for the championship.

Unfortunately, the Tectapers were ready to play their best ball of the season and swept the Popeye Nine in the playoffs. They had added a fiercesome bat in the lineup in Carmine Scocca. And Tectape's manager Perri hoped veteran slugger Horace Lybrand would continue his torrid hitting volley.

Division Champs	
Senior	The Royals
Industrial	Tectapers
Community	Popeye Nine

Another Royal Fiasco for Tectape
Champs Keep the Industrial Leader Off Base

54

And so, the Royals took on Tectape for the 1954 Championship.

Things looked bright for Tectape. They took Game One. A spark was Carmine Scocca who belted a homer and a double to boost the Tapers. Jabbo Shelton and Earl Williams each had two hits for the Royals. It was pitcher Danny Brandon who garnered the win for Tectape.

Resting Brandon for Game Two played into the Royals advantage as they ran away with a punishing win. It came down to Game Three to decide who was best in New Rochelle

A competitive Perri matched strategies with Will Richardson. Now in his 40s, Richardson coached and played. His goal was to keep Tec off the bases Perri's plan was to keep Shelton hitless. Neither strategy worked well, and it was defense that ultimately decided the series. The Royals fielders made the right throws and squelched rallies.

So 1954 belonged to the Royals, although Tectape placed a valiant second. The Tapers could only take solace that there was always next year. As always, next year looked so far away when looking ahead from the remaining days of summer. It was much like Vito Valentinetti's long walk from the mound in Chicago that early spring day in 1954, when the Yankees bats spoiled his debut.

Baseball had its heartbreaks, and even softball could prove hard. Perri's tape had run out for the year, but the Tectapers would "someday" find a place in the sun.

Vanishing Desoto

It was one of the classic brands of the 1950s. The Desoto was made by Chrysler from 1928 to 1961. The car's logo featured the image of Hernando de Soto, whose conquistador helmet donned some hood ornaments. Known as the main advertiser on Groucho Marx TV show "You Bet Your Life," it was also Mr. Cunningham's family car on "Happy Days." But tastes were changing and the popularity of the car began to ebb mid-decade. In many ways 1954 was the last hurrah for cars featuring the famed explorer. A Desoto was turning into a dad car, and the flashy Chevy on its way to become the quintessential sporty car.

1955

Wicked Weather

55

Season Shortened by Squalls

Rained Out

As if digging a giant trench to create Interstate-95 wasn't disruptive enough for New Rochelle, the whole situation was exacerbated by treacherous weather, once-in-a-generation storms that flooded parts of the city. Many softball players became resigned to a shortened season with all the rainouts, thruway construction, and change in neighborhood boundaries.

Rough Surf

With Westchester weather stuck in higher-than-average territory, teams sweated out the summer of 1955 and kids flocked in droves to beaches at New Rochelle's Hudson Park and Glen Island and Manaroneck's Harbor Island.

The I-95 Trench

New York State contracted to establish a "super highway" through the heart of New Rochelle. Demolition and construction altered baseball schedules, garbage pickup, traffic patterns and school days. Shop owners fumed. Evictees protested amid a total lack of response to the chaos. Construction was delayed in the downtown because residents in private houses and apartments refused to vacate the premises. A belligerent locus was Harrison Street and Burling Lane where apartment dwellers refused to budge in the face of tractors.

PARKING PLAN RAILROADED BY NEW HAVEN-RR

In mid-summer, the New Rochelle City Council argued who had the right to charge fees for railroad parking. Councilman George Vergara challenged the railroad's request for an increase. A 1941 agreement said the city, not the New Haven Railroad, had the authority over parking, he claimed. Mayor Stanley Church stated his position was clear: commuters would not pay for parking, especially when no other communities on the rail line were paying fees. Apparently, America's growing love affair with the car was not shared by the railroad operators who wanted to sell tickets for cars too, even those standing still.

Talk of the Sound Shore

Sportsman-like

New Rochelle Police Headquarters in 1955 credited the local Little League with helping to sharply reduce juvenile delinquency in the Queen City of the Sound. Speaking to a local newspaper paper, detective Joe Riefenberger and lieutenant Lawrence Ruhl agreed: "We never have trouble with the boys who have interest in sports."

Drafted by NBA

Months before the National Basketball Association took to the hardwoods, there was positive news for New Rochelle. Jesse Arnelle, one of New Rochelle High School's 'greatest athletes,' was drafted by the National Basketball Association in 1955. Arnelle graduated from Penn State and was chosen by the Fort Wayne Pistons in the second round—the 13th player overall. Arnelle was 6'5, 220lbs.

Meet You at the Cabana

New Rochelle was still considered a summer destination in 1955. But private clubs were eager to buy up waterfront real estate. The city council that year considered approvals for a new beach and tennis club. The Greentree Club sought a permit to build on the former Hynes estate, a four-acre site along the Long Island Sound.

RKO AND LOEWS OFFER CINEMATIC ESCAPES

With the heat too much to handle that summer, many chose to escape to the movies. There was a wide choice of cinema at the area's movie houses. The Pelham Picture House's cozy theater offered James Stewart and June Allyson in "Strategic Air Command," the Parkway had "Blackboard Jungle," and RKO featured "Revenge of the Creature." The adventurous might opt for a double feature of fun with "Death Row" and "Naked Amazon" at Loew's.

Early Season: A Warrens' Rally

The Action Opened with a Surprise Win by the Curlers

Early Season Action:

It was what so many Twilight teams aimed to do -- beat the best. And in an early season surprise, the Curlers did just that. They knocked off the mighty Royals in the Senior Softball Division, 5 to 3.

The Curlers right fielder Carl Verusio connected for a grand slam off of Ollie Flowers in the bottom of the first inning. Slugger Penella and Ron Semenza also added to the offensive barrage for the Curlers.

Over in the Community Division, the Warrens scored four times in the fourth to lead their team over the Choppers, 7 to 3. Offensive stalwarts Nino Perrino and Cookie Norberto keyed the victory with Ernie Flowers spacing three hits. Gabe Carino took the loss.

In other contests, Feeney Park Boys Club edged the Gay Dome with Joe Lucia's single, reviving an inning with two outs on his team.

Things were heating up in the Senior Division of the Twilight League. The Bonefro Club, one of the oldest softball franchises, bowed to the Gotti Nine, 3 to 2. Pete Gillespie's homer marked the difference. Vin Connelly was outdueled by Frank Farucci. In the Industrial League, United stopped Tompkins, 11 to 2. Sal Caporale, one of the most durable pitchers in the league, spread out three singles for the win.

That same evening, softball action indicated it would be an interesting road to the championship. Joe Iarocci fired blanks against the Curlers, 6 to 0. Sammy Toma had two hits for the winning Gotti Nine. In other games, United toppled the Knights 8 to 3 with Ed Carafa providing the key offensive swings.

Pitcher Ernie Flowers of the Warrens outdueled Tom deJulio of Feeney Park as the Warrens continued their show of muscle.

Offensive stalwarts Nino Perrino and Cookie Norberto keyed the Warren's victory with Ernie Flowers spacing three hits.

Rematch: Royals vs. Tectape

Jabbo's Bat Kept the Challengers at Bay

55

After a patch of bad weather, the softball leagues recommenced. The Warrens continued winning with a trouncing of Feeney Park Boys' Club, 8 to 2. Hitting honors went to Sal Oliverio, the Warrens catcher, Nino Bombace, and Ken Nicsarato. Al Paolucci was the notable offense on the losing Feeney Park squad.

```
'The Warrens'
Bombace      1B
Lanza        2B
Nicara       SS
Brown        3B
Perrino      LF
C Norberto   CF
N Norberto   RF
Oliverios    C
E Flowers    P
```

Bonefro Club's pitcher Ace Sheehan kept Dasche's Nine in check, 3 to 1. At Moore Field, the Royals ho-hummed their way to a victory 7 to 2 over United. Turner Stroman paced the Royals going 3 for 4 with Brud Flowers notching the win.

An unusual game took place between Ft. Slocum and the EMBRA Hawks. The game was called after five innings. The EMBRA, trailing 8 to 0, so severely criticized the two umpires, Jack Murray and Seely Burigo that the game was stopped for "unsportsmanlike conduct." Pitcher Jack Barnum of Ft. Slocum was awarded the win. Catcher Pennington had two hits for Slocum and Barnum unleashed a grand slam.

In the first game of the 1955 City Championship the matchup was Dan Brandon going against Bob Simmons. The Royals scored quickly and went on to win the opener 4 to 2 with Jabbo Shelton providing the batting ballast.

In the second championship series game, the defending champ Royals, defeated Tectape by a score of 10 to 7. The contest was decided in the fifth inning when Jabbo bunted for a hit, advanced to third on Stroman's double and scored on a wild pitch. Roland Allen then knocked in Stroman with a single

The Royals kept the lead. During the game, Brud Flowers and Will Richardson also homered for the Royals.

Perhaps it was the atrocious weather in June and July which was highlighted by bizarre patterns of flooding in nine states that explains the failure of teams to mount a sustained attack on the Royals' tight reign on the softball scene. Or maybe, the Royals were just damn good. Tectape's defense fell apart. It spelled out another title flag for the Royals.

They made it look easy.

Community Matters
Game Theory and the Art of Sportsmanship

55

The key to learning is to make learning indistinguishable from play. When that's possible, then so is excellence. That said, you can't expect youngsters to readily invent their own sports games, rules and leagues and go on to draw the best lessons. Rules make it a sport!

One of the cornerstones making up the foundation of any community is the sense or feeling of fellowship with others as a result of sharing attitudes, interests and goals. This creation of similarity or identity forms the basis of "community" and culture itself. Sports can play a major role in this formation of identity and therefore can be set apart in the context of raising social values and responsibilities.

Within this framework, fast-pitch softball played a part in fostering a feeling of community during its era. What made New Rochelle a little different and abound with a high level of participation was the availability of a range of experiences in team play. Early on young boys and girls played games both individually and on teams.

Not everyone shared sports and game experiences in the same way, but a high percentage did, and it showed up in the exploits of local grammar school, high school, and college athletics. For New Rochelle's sports advocates this was something self-evident that required commitment to action rather than reverence for theory.

Organizations Honing Important Play

Big results are not always the result of big recreation department budgets. In the 1950s, dedication, goodwill and love of community helped organizations bring in a golden age in local sports.

Here are some anchors of the 1950s sports community in New Rochelle. Keep in mind, many of these lacked direct access to fields and facilities. Yet, each made it their business to find ways to make the most of local resources.

Boys & Girls Clubs had three New Rochelle units, Feeney Park, Southside, and Remington that offered sports programs for youth which fostered group competition and sharpened athletic and social skills.

Catholic Youth Organization (CYO) & other religous groups fostered interaction in the sports arena especially in baseball, basketball and football.

New Rochelle Recreation Department—organized leagues like fast-pitch Twilight, managed facilities and championed city involvement with sports and awarded trophies for outstanding performance on teams at annual ceremonies they found sponsorship for and managed.

The Games We Played

New Rochelle was a haven for sports play in the 1950s. Not all of it was organized. Some was ad hoc. Early on, boys and girls in some cases, played games which prepared them for participating in team sports.

Some sports didn't require a ball field or elaborate accoutrements. Some simply needed a wall:

Stickball was played with an old broomstick or bat, tennis ball or Spaldeen "Pinkie." Usually, it was a one-on-one competition but could include as many as three on a side. My friend John Lucadamo and I played one-on-one stickball every day in the summer. Some kids played with a strike zone drawn in chalk on a hard surface. However, more than likely, the strike zone was an honor system, where each pitch was called ball or strike by the pitcher. The New Rochelle schools or parks had few facilities for stickball. Columbus Field provided the best setup for the game. Foul lines were set beforehand by the players. There were stickball diamonds and exotic locations behind such schools as Jefferson, Ward, Holy Family and Blessed Sacrament near Maple Avenue.

I can recall one of the longest stickball games in history when a match between George Borrelli and myself lasted 16 innings. The contest began in the sunshine and came to a close over three-and-a-half hours later, amidst the appearance of a highly dangerous lightning storm. I recall regulars like Shep and Archie from another side of town playing frequently during evening hours. One summer, Nello Amori organized a stickball league for Columbus School.

Then there was Stoopball. This game, played like baseball, was a lot of fun without a bat. A Spaldeen was used. And the "batter" would stay up until he was "struck out." The batter would throw the ball at a low angle against the "point" of the wall or building to a predetermined distance to mark as a single, double, triple or home run. If the defense caught the thrown ball, it was considered an out. The game was played almost always by grammar school kids. It was a skill to keep the ball in bounds. Of course, everyone tried to hit the point with sufficient force for a home run. It should also be pointed out that the offensive player did not have to hit the "point" but could also hit the ground or bounce the ball in front of the wall at a sufficient angle to create the height and distance to score. A dropped ball by a defender constituted a hit at whatever distance contact occurred.

Fantasy whiffleball was something Lou Bonomo and I created -- complete with a fictitious teams complete with rosters. The competition ended abruptly with the score tied in the championship game. With the bases full, I hit Lou's pitch and the ball splintered in two. One half sent past him for a game winning hit. The other was caught as the final out. After arguing the point for 15 minutes, the league was disbanded.

Marble Blast and Links

On the same day season openers were played at City Park and Moore Field, the Cross County Golf Range at California Road opened up for business, advertising "day and evening golf" and promising to improve your score. At the same time the annual marble tournament was held at Columbus School for kids of all ages.Bobby Newman captured the marble title and Lester Harris took the junior title in a competition involving 300 participants. During the 50's marbles rivalled Hide-and-Seek and Monopoly as pastimes among youngsters.

1956

The Short Stops

Pat Mandarano was a Paragon for Future Short Stops

56

Luis Aparicio was a rookie with the White Sox in 1956. He was also one of the last shortstops whose fielding ability alone made him a star. He put the "go" in the pennant winning 1959 ChiSox with his nonpareil defensive skills and speed on the base paths.

Times were changing, and a new model of shortstop that had yet to emerge in the Big Leagues was making himself known as he rose in the ranks at local ball fields. Fast-pitch softball was at the fore of this.

One of the impressive shortstops in the fast-pitch-softball leagues of the 1950s was Pat Mandarano. Compared to the Aparicio model, Mandarano was the paragon for future shortstops. Mandarano was big, bold, and rangy. In short, he was a short stop who brought massive offensive capability from behind a bat. He was more focused on the long ball. This more modern type of shortstop aided a batting order. He also suitably fit an evolving infield, which now used greater amounts of artificial turf and cultured landscaping, changing the nature of a batted ball's bounce.

While no one would call a defensive star like Aparicio a dinosaur, the fact was that among shortstops, one would see fewer and fewer slow rollers. Newer field configurations and turf compositions enabled bigger players to handle the position more efficiently. When a batter strikes a softball, it creates a faster moving spheroid. Today's shortstop is more likely to field in the gaps to cover such projectiles.

Mandarano played for the Paris Rogues (and was one of several brothers playing on the club). Pat was one of the top hitters in the fast-pitch era. His offensive strength shone as he led hitting for several title-bound teams throughout the 1950s.

Other standout shortstops included Al Ryder(Tectape) Charlie Billups (Royals), Jimmy Sabia and John DeMasi (Popeyes), Mike Merigliano (Knights), and Sal Sclafani (Strobls).

A ballplayer handling this position in fast-pitch had to take a leadership role in tightening up the infield and providing for defense up the middle. Any team tightening the gaps would carry a distinct advantage into the season, as Mandarano's many post-season outings attest.

1956:   *Talk of the Town in New Rochelle*   **56**

Andrea Doria Sinks

On July 25th, the Italian luxury-liner Andrea Doria slammed into a Swedish vessel en route to New York. The sinking Andrea Doria carried six passengers from New Rochelle. Breaking news bulletins were rare in 1956, but regular programming was interrupted. John Tillman of WPIX -TV 11 in New York covered the story with live interviews as helicopters brought back film footage. And NY's Channel 5, a Dumont station, conducted phone interviews with experts. New Yorkers tuned in with both trepidation and curiosity.

Some 50 passengers perished the next morning when Andrea Doria capsized. It was the biggest story of the summer and folks attending the ball games of the Twilight league talked about it incessantly. Part of that was interest in six New Rochelleans who were onboard and were among the 1,600 survivors.

Yonkers Raceway

The month of August meant a couple of things for local players: It was now "post time." Yonkers Raceway was opening for the season In fact, at Yonkers, the next 105 nights were touted as "opening night." Still, the "first" opening night drew an amazing 23,000 attendees who watched a filly named Newton Gal place first for a lucky $13 payout.

BUDGETARY BOOST FOR SCHOOLS

New Rochelle city planners, claiming school enrollments were expected to rise 47 percent over ten years, received approval to spend $9.9 million to fund an expansion of the high school, create a new elementary school and a junior high. The baby boomers were being felt.

AN APOLOGY FROM WALTER'S HOT DOGS

Founded in 1919, Walter's Hot Dogs of Mamaroneck was always a treat. But the dragon-domed dog shop apologized for raising prices of frankfurters to 20 cents with an advert in the Standard Star in 1956. Luckily, 35 cents still bought two franks garnished with special relish .

Pitching at 125-mph
The Royals Looked in Peak Form

56

The prelude to the 1956 Twilight League Season followed a pattern that shows just how seriously local players took their game. Typically, the windmill pitchers in early season were ahead of the hitters. It took time for batters to size up these rocket launchers. As one batter put it: "A fast-pitch softball comes in on a batter at the equivalent of 125-mph, requiring a more rapid response than hardball thrown in the majors." Thus batting practice was a necessity and continued well into the actual start of the season.

This year was no different. After some mismatches in the previous season, league planners continued there endless tinkering aimed at balancing game play between the divisions -- Senior, Industrial and Community.

And they certainly got things right in 1956 when the Recreation Department put the Royals in the Senior Division, amongst other veteran clubs.

Once again, the venerable Royals were at the pinnacle, and teams vying to reach that level sought to stock their rosters with proven performers. After all the Brooklyn Dodgers reached the top with their world series upset in 1955, so anything was possible!

Maybe. In their first main skirmish, the Royals looked in peak form, pounding the Knights 8 to 0, with a reliable Bobby Simmons throwing tireless barrages. That evening, each of these Royals garnered two hits: Ed Green, Charlie Billups, and Will Richardson.

If New Rochelle had a single sports dynasty, its name would have been the Royals.

No team won as many league championships as the Royals did during the 1950s

The term "dynasty" was hardly pushed by the team. Yet the result of season after season of winning came as no more surprise than surprise than the Yankees winning a pennant.

Dynasty was a moniker well deserved by the Royals and staff. Orchestrating a beautiful balance of offense and defense, the team met its expectations. And like Mickey Mantle who would hit on all cylinders in achieving the triple crown in 1956 and Don Larsen in reaching for perfection in the World Series, the Royals were as perfect as you could get.

Who Knew Blue Could Be Royal?
The Royals Were the Team to Beat

The blue-uniformed Royals were a tight-knit team.

Though identified with the 1950s, their winning tradition dated back to the 1940s. The record shows they won over ten city championships as well as their share of softball tournaments, playing the fast-pitch variety of the game.

Amazingly, they won the close games as well as the blowouts during their reign. They played with quiet precision. Their credo was: "make fewer mistakes than your opponent."

The Royals started playing together in 1945. They were known then as the Junior Yankees, later the Yankees. Their main nemesis in the WWII era was a team known as the Green Wave.

The two teams decided to merge as the Royals. From the Green Wave, they picked up four of their best players: pitcher Bobby Simmons, first baseman Turner Stroman, catcher Earl Williams, and second baseman Rudy Kemp.

Already on the team were all the Flowers brothers, Horace Lybrand, Will Richardson Frank Thomas, Cliff Shelton, and Harry Johnson. Shortly after WWII,

Bill Marino joined. The leader for the Royals was the oldest of the Flowers Family- Brud. His athletic career began as a lightweight boxer - a very successful one.

The majority of their players came from the Remington area also known as the "Hollow" to some. Marino, their one-armed pitcher, joined the Royals mainly because he grew up in neighboring Remington.

They were guided through the years by Brud Flowers. But the person who was day-to-day manager was Will Richardson. Will manned center-field usually chewing a wad of Redman tobacco mix. Will batted right handed and was an excellent line-drive hitter. The core of their offense was Turner Stroman. This first baseman with bat arched high was a menacing sight and rightfully so. He was consistently effective, hitting for a high batting average and long ball. To top things off, the team had two catchers. Earl Williams and Pint Murray who were like coaches on the field and kept things moving.

The Royals were the team to beat. And in 1956, even the top contenders were but hopefuls for the crown.

Remembering Old Windmillers

Old-Timers Day, 1956

56

The New York Yankees had an Old-Timers Day. And if it was a good enough idea for the House that Ruth built, then it was good enough for New Rochelle players, the local recreation department figured.

Except, New Rochelle did it differently. The annual match pitted old timers against the new kids on the block. The 1956 game would see the Feeney Park Alumni Team play a current club. In attendance were a group of all-star pitchers past and present, a gathering of greats to play a benefit match for the Boys & Girls Clubs of New Rochelle. Four of the top softball pitchers in the metropolitan area would demonstrate the art of windmill softball.

The first was Joe Connolly of New Rochelle who had played 11 years for the Bonefro Club. Connolly was a master of many speeds and showed pinpoint control with his windmill pitches.

Another was "Chick" Talgo from Mamaroneck. Talgo had been a mainstay in Jones Beach Summer League, known as a "drop pitch" specialist.

A legend of the mound, "Rush" Riley of Pelham was also onboard the veteran squad. A fireballing righty, Riley started his fast-pitch softball career in 1939. He also held the unofficial record of pitching the most games in a season, sometimes playing games back to back since he was so sought after in tournament play.

Then there was the Royals "Ace," Bobby Simmons. He was a steady veteran who had played for a dozen years for New Rochelle's top Twilight Team and no doubt contributed to the Royals' remarkable record of success.

It may have been a benefit game, but these competitive players knew how to put on a show for local fans as they wound the windmill.

Saccone's Legendary Lemon Ice

Pits Included at No Extra Charge

During the 1950s it was New Rochelle's most famous shack, home to an enduring local legend called Saccone's Lemon Ice. Located on Sixth Street at the intersection of Washington Avenue, Saccone's still exists today, but its original wooden structure is long gone, replaced by a more permanent stucco-coated digs where the mystique remains. Not far from New Rochelle's Columbus Field, Saccone's was a local favorite of Twilight League ballplayers and just about everyone else.

Sure there were other lemon ice stands, but owner Nunzio Saccone left his mark on New Rochelle by raising his craft to an art form. This was the real deal. "Nunzi," as he was called, would go down to the Terminal Market near Yankee Stadium to buy the freshest lemons and sugar by the sack. But what made Saccone's different was Nunzi's method. No machine was used. Instead, Saccone would whittle down giant blocks of ice and then hand shave the final product. More often than not, you might find yourself sucking on an actual lemon pit that made its way through a laborious shaving process. But if anyone dare complained to Nunzi, he never changed his method. Authenticity sometimes comes with the pits included.

If the 1950s were the Golden Age for fast-pitch softball then Saccone also made it the golden era of lemon ice. There was an air of mystery over the formula. Sure, the ingredients were a given, but in what proportion? Saccone had the mix just right. And his secret formula was as sought after as Coca Cola's. But whereas Coke was mass produced and available everywhere, Saccone's work was hand produced and available only at a single wooden shack "Up the West."

Saccone served ice in waxy-paper cups with much aplomb at a 10 cents a piece. On his busiest summer day he might sell close to 500 such cups of lemon ice that were typically "squeezed" until the very last bit of lemon ice rose from this makeshift pop-up to hit the palette. Those who unwisely failed to savor the taste and instead guzzled were treated to a brain freeze. Lemon Ice was the best bargain in town. It was also the best – and only – item on Saccone's menu.

For Twilight Leaguers, finishing a summer game at Columbus Field, a trip down the street to the shack was an unspoken must. Lemon ice and baseball— they fit together perfectly!

Dining Out "Up the West"

The idea of casual dining had not yet fully arrived in New Rochelle, even by the mid-1950s. The Golden Arches had not extended its reach this far east and "fastfood" was not a household word unless you were talking about using an iron to make grilled cheese sandwiches or something like a Belgian Waffle.

Adventurous players seeking to eat after a game at Columbus Field had the option of choosing between a triumvirate of non-gourmet food. (The term gourmet was equally unknown in that era, and players likely thought "Gourmet" were a couple of singers named Steve and Edie.)The first option was not gourmet, but it was fast – Saccone's. And those who chose the second option were sure to talk about it – and likely still are 60 years later. "Millie's" was a delicatessen in West New Rochelle that might later have served as a movie set aimed at showing what a 1950s store looked like. It was boxy place with wooden shelves that stacked to the ceiling, a counter topped with barrel-sized mustard and mayonnaise containers, and a long linoleum-covered hallway, in the back, that led to an adjoining apartment where Millie actually lived when not working.

In New Rochelle, no one calls a sandwich a "sandwich." To this day, the local term is "Wedge" (as in a long bread roll with a wedge sliced out), a phrase still used on the eastern shore of the Long Island Sound between the Bronx and Greenwich, Connecticut. Millie's wedges remain some of the largest in recorded history. Either Millie's scale was broken or she simply couldn't be bothered to measure cold cuts that were stuffed into sandwiches, literally by the pound. As amazing as this was, it wasn't the most remarkable thing about Millie's vaunted wedges. Just as Saccone couldn't be bothered to eliminate pits from ices, Millie saved time by not removing the wax paper covering that sheathed cold cuts when she sliced ham or cheese. The net result was that sandwiches came coated with a thin coating of deli wax-paper on the edges of ham or cheese slices.

It's a Wedge, Not a Sandwich!

The third West New Rochelle dining option was one of the most popular, an eatery known as Vaccaro's. Half pizza parlor and half restaurant, the two wings were divided by wall with a small bar window for delivering drinks or pitchers of soda. Most remarkable, Vaccarro's was home of the 50-cent pizza. That was for the whole pie, not just a slice.

Though post-game eating options were limited around Columbus Field, other baseball venues were worse. At best, you might occasionally have a Good Humor truck show up. Usually, it was "Pete" the Good Humor Man "at your service."

While self aware New Rochelleans loved their wedges, they always quashed newcomers use of the term "hero" or "sub," which to local ears still sounds offensive. In addition to Millie's other prominent places to "grab a wedge" in 1956 included Sacco's, Mirabella's and Caruso's in the West End. Salerno's served wedges on Main Street. Johnny's was on Weyman Avenue. Beechmont Deli was near the high school. Vin Lou's was next to the old Chase Bank on North Avenue, and Lanza's resided next to City Park.

So who was best? Overall, Millie's wins in terms of "value added." If you wanted mayo for example, Millie's always managed to get some mustard mixed in from the massive condiment jars she kept on the counter. Millie was ahead of her time when it comes to services offered. If she trusted you, you could ask her to put it on your tab -- no credit scores or finance charges involved, just a little more provolone thanks to Millie. At most she might scribble a note to herself on a brown paper bag that served as her adding machine.

During the early Cold War, there were other reasons to love Millie's. Her wedges were so big, you were safe in case of a nuclcar attack. One wedge could feed a family of four for a whole week.

Bonnies Blast Ahead
Bonefro Club Battles Strobl's

As the season moved along, the Bonefro Club "Bonnies" edged Strobl's - 6 to 4 - who then fell to third place. Manager Bert Terranova of the Bonnies called on ace right-hander Lou Piedmont to take on Strobl's. (sponsored by a namesake bar and grill then located on the northbound side of the New Rochelle Train Station.)

Bonefro set their sight on the first place Paris Rogues and expected their hitters to carry them to the top - sluggers like Lou Guida, Frank Pensella, Sal Sclafani, and Junior Santora. A matchup was just a few weeks away.

Meanwhile, the Blue Birds coasted to five-straight wins as pitcher Bob Becker scattered five hits at Jefferson Field as the taxi men beat Bonefro. Ben Uzzillo paced the birds with three hits.

Elsewhere, Don Summo, a consistent workhorse for Paris Rogues, won his fourth game holding off the Popeyes, 2 to 1.

Next, the Paris Rogues tripped up the Spartans largely due to Cookie Norberto's long-ball power and some timely hitting by the Mandarano Brothers. In other early season contests, the gold-and-black clad Warrens stopped the Popeye Nine on Nino Perrino's single.

Just starting their second round play, Strobl's, competing in the Senior League, defeated the hard hitting Knights 4 to 2 with Marty Colombo as the winning pitcher and hitting honors going to Mike Merigliano and the two Franks (Fodora and Mucci).

Meanwhile, Bonefro Club was gaining momentum as they utilized Vin Connolly their ace to face Strobl's. Connolly delivered and boosted the Bonnies in the standings. They crushed Strobl's 10 to 0 with Connolly leading the offense with a 4-for-4 night. Sil Burigo and Al Ryder contributed two hits, each.

It was a bad July for Strobl's. The defending champs, the Royals won 7 to 3 with Jabbo Shelton having the hot bat, 4-for-4, along with Will Richardson who collected two doubles. As the second round began the Royals tapped Simmons to face Bonefro. Despite Pete Gillespie's three hits, Bonefro could not contain the Royals who won, 5 to 2. Simmons' sinker worked well as he got the Bonnies to hit 15 groundouts. Rudy Kemp provided firepower for the Royals in their victory.

Next Up, the Paris Rogues
Meet the Mandaranos -- Half-a-Team's Worth

The Paris Rogues extended their streak to six wins as they pounded the BlueBirds, 8 to 1. Donald Summo twirled a two hitter.

Speculation was growing for a confrontation between the Senior League leaders, the Royals and the Community League's waxing Rogues.

The Paris lineup was as formidable as any in the circuit. It was loaded with Mandaranos: Mandarano at first base, second, and third as well as left field. Add in sluggers Cookie Norberto, Jake Cassara and catcher Skip Martin. This was one potent offense.

The Mandaranos alone were quite a marvel. Pat played multiple positions including catcher and was one of the league's top hitters. Tut was a solid infielder and a steady line-drive hitter. Al was an outfielder who could also go long.

John Mandarano was primarily a third baseman who played a dangerous halfway between third and home plate.

He played so close to the batter -- as a matter of fact -- that he held his glove over his face and peeked through the fingers of his glove to watch plays. If it was aimed to intimidate, it usually worked.

At Columbus Field, Ken Necerato of the Paris hit a three-run homer to vanquish Sycamore Athletic Club, 3 to 1.

The Paris Rogues were on the stepping stone of softball history with the chance to become only the second team to go a regular season undefeated since the 1947 Plywoodies. Remarkably, Pat and Tut Mandarano were players on both Paris and Plywoodies! Call it Manadaranos revenge.

The Mandaranos alone were quite a marvel

This was not the only industrial development on the table. In the Industrial League, underrated Bob Mittelstat hurled a two hitter to propel the Splicers past Fort Slocum.

Slocum had lost its first game of the year but remained in first place. Later in the week, Dan Brandon fired a no hitter against a suddenly struggling Slocum squad.

Paris Rogues Unbeaten
First Team Undefeated in Regular Season Since 1947

56

The reigning champs were on a roll too. The Royals erupted for 11 hits and beat Strobls. Brud Flowers picked up the win while Richardson and Stroman stroked three hits each. Although their explosiveness at bat was well documented, the part of the game which elevated their performance was in a word defense. The Royals were kings of keeping rivals off the bases.

The Paris Rogues, meanwhile, on their way to a record, ran into trouble. Paris had fallen behind Popeye Nine 4 to 1 at the end off the third inning. Clutch hits by Jake Cassara, Donnie Zack, and Cookie Norberto led a turnaround in favor of Paris. Rally completed, they became the first team since 1947 to finish the regular season unbeaten.

Tectape clinched the Industrial League title with a 4 to 1 victory over the Splicers. Pitching ace Brandon earned the Tapers the right to play the Royals for the city championship. To date, the Royals winning record extended for ten consecutive years. But in a year where tradition in baseball took a hit with the loss of the great Connie Mack, Tectape also was hoping

Rush Riley Pulls a Royal Upset

Taking a break from usual league play, the Royals entered Pelham's County Invitational Tourney along with some local teams.

The Royals may have been the favorite, but with more than a little help from legendary "Rush" Riley, a less-known Lauricella's of Pelham dethroned New Rochelle royalty, 2 to 1. Under blazing skies at Hutchinson Field, Pelham carried the day with Tony Zimbalatti's batting.

Riley fanned six and walked one in the contest while coming off a relief stint against Eastchester earlier in thesame day. Former Iona standout Hank Marusells drove in the winning tally.

tradition would travel in a different direction.

Once again, Tectape would find itself battling the Royals for the championship title of the Twilight League.

Miracle Comeback
One of the Great Fast-Pitch Games of the Decade

On the first Saturday in September with football waiting in the wings, the Royals and Tectape squared off for the fast-pitch championship. In a rather matter-of-fact approach, the Royals blanked the Tapers 3 to 0 with a tight defense, solid pitching and timely hitting. Bobby Simmons notched another playoff win and shut down the Tapers with two hits. Game Two had the Royals on the verge of their 11th straight city title. No city sports team ever approached those numbers. Tectape was not ready to give up.

Going into the fifth inning, Tape held a 10-3 advantage. The Royals being the erstwhile champion bounced back and did so against one of the best in the league--Dan Brandon. First, Jabbo Shelton singled. Al Flowers reached base on an infield error. Then, it was Will Richardson's turn. With two strikes on him, Richardson lined a base hit to center, scoring in Shelton. Bruce Flowers drew a walk. Roland Allen beat out an infield hit to make it 10-5.Charlie Billups, the shortstop laced into a tired Dan Brandon pitch and drove it to deep left for one of the most dramatic homers in many a year!

The Royals were now just a run away.

Manager Mario Perri of the Tapes still stuck with Brandon who got out of jams throughout the year. Brandon wanted to soldier on and Perri did not fight it. Horace Lybrand the veteran lefty swinger singled up the middle just beyond Ryder's reach. Shelton then scored the tying run on a Simmons' "Texas leaguer" to right. It was as if some terrible jinx had befallen the Tapesters. Perri was speechless.

As skies darkened, the game ended 10-10. It capped off one of the great games of the decade.

Tape was "psyched out" because of the Royals miracle comeback.

The final game of the championship softball series was at City Park. Like a rerun of a Twilight Zone episode, it was Jabbo Shelton's quiet single which broke a 2-2 tie and eventually spelled the end of the Tapers annual run. In defeat, Will Archer played exceptionally well. Sports reporter Jim O'Toole summed up the Royal's stunning performance:

"New Rochelle could not have a better team to represent us..."

Post-Game Show
Sports Happenings After Twilight Play

56

```
New Rochelle High Football
Schedule for 1956
9/21 Blessed Sacrament
9/30 Mount Saint Michael
10/6 Glen Cove
10/13 Stepinac
10/20 NYMA
10/26 White Plains
11/23 Iona Prep
```

```
Iona Prep Football
Schedule for 1956
9/30 St. Francis
10/7 Mount Saint Michael
10/20 Chaminade
10/26 Stepinac
11/3 Xavier
11/11 Cardinal Hayes
11/23 New Rochelle
```

```
Blessed Sacrament Football
Schedule for 1956
9/21  New Rochelle
10/6  Harrison
10/13 Bronxville
10/20 Rye
10/27 Pelham
11/3  Cardinal Farley
11/10 Tuckahoe
11/22 St. Mary's
```

Duel Worth the Wait

An historic matchup of two legendary Babe Ruth League pitchers - Gigi Amorsano versus Don Lamparella - took place in 1956.

Lamparella took the mound for the New Rochelle Yanks and Amorsano toiled for the New Rochelle Bears. It didn't take long for one team to strike. In the bottom of the first inning, the Yanks slugger Frank "Cindy" Nardozzi walloped a homer to deep center off Amorsano to give the Yanks a 2-to-0 lead.

Amorsano would then allow only four hits while Lamparella permitted two.

Gold Medal

News came in from the Summer Olympics in Melbourne, Australia that New Rochelle native Lou Jones was a gold medal winner in the 400-meter relay. Jones had previously set a racing record for the same event at Olympic trials in Los Angeles. This local Olympian later coached track and field for New Rochelle High School.

1957

Team Profile

Popeye Nine

Spinach Men

Colors:
Red and White

Home Base:
West New Rochelle

Ace Pitchers:
Dorme and Mercurio

Key Players:
Ariginello, Dorme, Gallo, Giordano,
Sabia, Telesco

Manager:
Popeye Claps

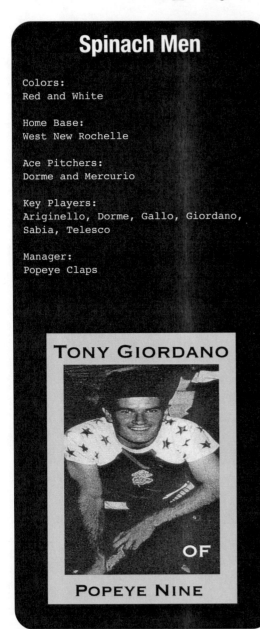

TONY GIORDANO

OF

POPEYE NINE

Box Score

The Popeye Nine was a perennial underdog team that swept an amazing 22-games in a row in the 1957 Season on their path to a title shot.

Though they lost that tight contest, the Popeyes remained one of the most popular teams of the era thanks to avid support from West New Rochelle fans that saw them as their adopted home team.

They were previously known as the Scorpions (and then Orioles) before namesake coach "Popeye" Claps chose a moniker that stuck. Some players would depart to form a team called the Frosts in the latter part of the decade.

The team boasted excellent pitching from Dorme and Mercurio and an air-tight defensive team.

Team Profile

Royals

Kings of the Diamond

Colors:
Blue and White

Home Base:
Players came primarily from the
Lincoln, Remington, City Park areas
of New Rochelle.

Ace Pitchers:
Bill Marino and Bobby Simmons

Key Players:
Stroman, Simmons, Shelton, Richardson

Manager:
Bruce "Brud" Flowers

BRUCE FLOWERS

THE ROYALS

Flowering of a Dynasty

The Royals comprised one of the great dynasties in fast-pitch softball history, winning all 1950s local championship titles, save two. One was because the team opted out of the finale to play in a tournament outside of New Rochelle. In the 1940's the Royals merged with a team known as the Green Wave and began their long run of city championships. They were the benchmark against which all great windmill teams were measured. Having served their country heroically in World War II, members of this predominately black team were led by battling Brud Flowers, a professional boxer in the 1940s. The team was known for its unwillingness to commit defensive errors, while exploiting even the smallest mistake by competitors. New Rochelle dedicated city park field to Flowers after his death in 1979.

Team Profile

Tectape

Industrial Giant

Colors:
Orange, Gray and White

Home Base:
Employees of the Tuck Tape Industries

Ace Pitcher:
Danny Brandon

Key Players:
Bohn (of), Ryder (1b), Brandon (p),
Hollis (p)

Coach:
Mario Perri

AL RYDER

1 B

TECTAPE

Tale of the Tape

The Champions of Twilight League play in 1958 and 1959 were the men of Tectape. Under ultra-competitive coach Mario Perri, Tectape was the archetypal success story of commercial-sponsored play on the fields of New Rochelle's Twilight League of the 1950s.

Players were almost exclusively employees of Tuck Tape Industries an adhesives manufacturer. This fact that bred both camaraderie and competitiveness. Their most valuable player was workhorse pitcher Danny Brandon who contributed to their dual championship wins and many near-successes throughout the 1950s. Late in the decade, pitcher Lee Hollis joined, augmenting the depth of the team's pitching arsenal.

Team Profile

Bonefro

Bonnies

Colors:
Black and White

Home Base:
South End and West New Rochelle

Ace Pitcher:
Piedmont, Summo, Joe Connelly, Vin Connelly

Key Players:
Burigo, Semenza, Summo and Connelly

DONALD SUMMO

P

BONEFRO

Pitching Dynamo

The Bonnies won a number of divisional titles in New Rochelle's Twilight League in the 1950s. The club was known for exceptional and hitting and pitching. In 1953, the club boasted an impressive 14-game win streak. In fact, the Bonnies were a recognized contender in nearly every season thereafter.

The Bonnies are the most notable example of a Twilight League team sponsored by a local social club that saw sports as a vital part of a healthy community . Its patron Bonefro Club, then located off of North Avenue in New Rochelle.

For some Bonnies, play was not a simple matter of recreation. Its roster of players included Sil Burigo who would later go pro after being signed by the Bristol Owls minor league team.

Team Profile

Forresters

Tenacious Woodsmen

Colors:
Green and White

Home Base:
Union Ave.

Ace Pitcher:
Efferen and Woodell

Key Players:
Merigliano, Efferen, Focazio

MIKE MERIGLIANO

SS

FORRESTERS

Team of Contrasts

Another team from the western part of the city, the Forresters Club was located on Union Avenue. They were a team of contrasts comprised of the oldest pitching staff in the Twilight League mixed with a team of youngsters.

The Forresters were consistent winners. They made it to the championship series in 1958 Season where they fell short to Tectape.

A scrappy, grind it out type of team, they were lead by feisty shortstop Mike Merigliano and colorful catcher George " Pencil" Pierro through the decade.

Also onboard was a steady right hander veteran player "Woody" Woodell, who was in his fifties in the 1950s, making him one of the longest running Twilight League players of the era.

Team Profile

Rogues

Paris Rogues

Colors:
Purple and White

Home Base:
Grove Street

Ace Pitcher:
Summo

Key Players:
Mandarano Brothers(John,Tut,and Pat),
Norberto

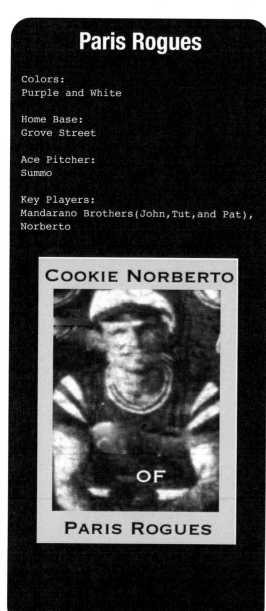

COOKIE NORBERTO

OF

PARIS ROGUES

Brothers Mandarano

The Paris Rogues was one of the Twilight League's most dangerous teams. When at full strength, their offense was formidable. As if the Mandarano Brothers weren't enough to worry about, add Cookie Norberto and you had power to spare. The rogues held the record for consecutive wins. Pitcher Donald Summo hurled more innings than anyone in the league. Mandarano exhibited utter confidence, intimidating batters by positioning himself half-way betwixt third base and home plate. It might seem over the top, but this was the Rogues' brash style.

Also known as the Paris Shoppes the team was sponsored by a discount clothier on Grove Street.

Fast-Pitch
1950s
Trading Cards

JIMMY SABIA

POPEYE NINE

DONALD SUMMO

BONEFRO

MIKE MERIGLIANO

FORRESTERS

RONALD SEMENZA

BONEFRO

Fast-Pitch
1950s
Trading Cards

MARIO PERRI

COACH

TECTAPE

BILLY BOHN

OF

TECTAPE

AL RYDER

1B

TECTAPE

BILL MARINO

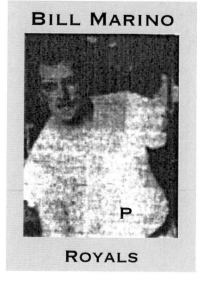

P

ROYALS

Fast-Pitch
1950s

Trading Cards

COOKIE NORBERTO

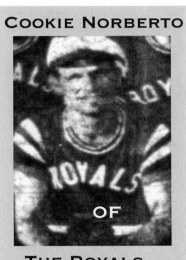

THE ROYALS

TURNER STROMAN

THE ROYALS

BOB SIMMONS

THE ROYALS

BRUCE FLOWERS

THE ROYALS

GAME OF THE DECADE

The Fastpitch softball game of the decade for the 1950s was a classic showdown between Twilight League heavyweights -- Tectape and the Royals.

It happened in 1956, during a championship face-off -- a game where both teams were in such top form that the game ended in a rare draw.

The action matched pitcher Bob Simmons of the Royals against Tectape's Dan Brandon. Both were in peak shape, but each team had the batting skills to counter their fast arms.Tectape had much to prove. For the previous three years running, Tectape had made it into the championship series only to be bested by the Royals. Now it was Game Two of a three-game series in which the Royals were ahead with one win.

Things were looking good for Tectape. It was the fifth inning and the Tapers held a comfortable lead of 10 to 3. Brandon was the ace on the mound and his arm seemed to be holding up as his team headed for a win. However, the Royals were not going down without a fight. In single inning, the bottom of the fifth, the Royals managed to score seven runs. This included a grand slam by Charlie Billups who caught one of Brandon's changeups and blasted out of City Park. In the same inning, Horace Lybrand singled to get the tying run -- leaving the score 10 to 10.

It had been a remarkable game. Umpires called it a draw as dusk descended, making further play impossible. This after all was the "Twilight League" and field lights were still far in the future.

Tectape proved its strength in Game Two, but the Royals could find ways to win that often seemed as miraculous as well as skillful. They would go on to win the series in Game Three.

New Rochelle's
Talk of the Town

1957

Main Street, New Rochelle

In New Rochelle that August, shoppers were still committed and attuned to spending their disposable income locally. The venerable Colony Shop on Main Street held a smoke sale and attracted lines of people over three blocks long. Congestion was such that police let people in the store one at a time to avoid chaos. The flourishing downtown, one of the oldest in the nation peaked in the 1950s, its last hurrah before a more car-centric economy would birth regional malls, leading to a decline of its once-famed Main Street shopping district.

American Bandstand

As those dogged days of August rolled around in 1957, Dick Clark was introduced to America. On the new show, "American Bandstand" Clark hosted dance shows which featured Paul Anka, the Dubs, Lee Andrews and the Hearts, Jerry Lee Lewis, and a group known as the Tunedrops -- all during that first month. The Mount Vernon native did the show from Philadelphia and became an American icon.

Twilight League pitchers quickly adopted Lee's "Great Balls of Fire" as their theme song for the remainder of the decade.

1957: Softball-Sized Sputnik Launches Soviet Space Race

TOSCANINI DIES

World renowned conductor Arturo Toscanini passed away in 1957. His grandson, Wilfredo, a resident of New Rochelle, recounted his grandfather's lifetime achievements in the local newspaper, the Standard Star.

DODGERS "GO WEST"

In May, the baseball world was shaken by Walter O'Malley's announcement he would move the Brooklyn Dodgers to Los Angeles. Soon the Giants would follow, going west. The era of mobility had left its mark on America's pastime.

A Classic Season for Twilighters
Setting the Stage with Warm Up Play

It was the late spring. But it felt more like the summer in New Rochelle. The mercury far exceeded seasonal norms. It was now May. And a young man's fancy turned to one-of-two perennial and consuming pastimes: local beauties or baseball. More often than not, it was both, sometimes providing a competition in its own right as far as time was concerned.

That said, 1957 was an iconic year that recalls more than just memorable bezels and fins of two-tone-color Chevies that debuted on roadways. Turquoise and creamy white were the favorite colors at local dealerships. And they brightened the thoroughfares of New Rochelle like a fleet of exclamation marks that suggested confidence and youthful optimism about the future.

With the help of ads featuring Dinah Shore, the image of these classic Chevies was inexorably linked to homemade apple pie and baseball. Parking lots, before and after games, featured these steely beauties with AM radios blaring, sometimes staticky, renditions of pop hits like Elvis' chart-topping "Jailhouse Rock" as well as tunes from Chuck Berry, Buddy Holly, and Jerry Lee Lewis. Nearby, teenagers on Main Street packed

movie theaters to view all-time classics such as "I Was A Teenage Werewolf, " "Jailhouse Rock," and "Rodan."

It was a golden age that celebrated youth. Yet, it was also the last summer in the age of innocence for America. In October, the U.S. status quo of presumed preeminence in all things was shattered, strangely enough, by a softball-sized object known as Sputnik that surfed the stratosphere.

But in May local ball players had more terrestrial things on their minds than the Soviet Union's aggressive pitch for space. Training began. And for the average player this consisted of shagging flyballs, batting practice and oiling gloves.

The latter involved enclosing one's leather mitt with a softball, after applying saddlesoap and wrapping the glove with rope or twine - hopefully stretching it back to shape after a winter storage.

Soon the stage would bet set for the 1957 season. And in the fast-pitch softball leagues, it was pitching staff that would again and again prove to be decisive...

The Amazing "Rush" Riley
The Pitcher Who Averaged Ten Games a Week

New Rochelle teams took part in county tournaments during the regular softball season. As a result, rosters often overlapped at the local and county levels.

At tournies we encounter one-- Don "Rush" Riley. A hired gun, Riley was a pitcher from Pelham who would bolster a great number of championship teams. He averaged an amazing ten games a week, sometimes playing in Mount Vernon in the morning and hurling at Jones Beach in the evening. Riley was a force of nature.

A graduate of Pelham High, he was an early devotee of softball legend Roy Stevenson. Rush himself became the stuff of local folklore. He was the standard against which all pitchers in Metro New York were compared.

As with wild west gunslingers, known for their speed and accuracy, rare pitchers like Riley could turn the tide of a game against almost any team.

It is a good comparison in that Riley did not always play for a single team but might be called in as a fast gun pitcher at a various local, county and even state tournaments held in the 1950s.

Even against the sometimes seemingly invincible, New Rochelle Royals, Riley might turn the tide. Such was the case when Riley led pitching for a small Pelham squad in 1956 called

He was the standard against which all pitchers in Metro New York were compared.

Lauricella's that bested the men in royal blue in what was the upset of the decade for some minds.

A rare sportsman, Riley threw at major league speeds and boasted an almost Olympic endurance on the mound. Not only did he not lag in later innings, he seemed to consistently thrive when called upon in the clutch. And that was true even in cases where it was his fourth game in just two days.

While there were other excellent pitchers in the Twilight Era, Riley's sheer speed, flamboyance and his decisive ubiquity in tournament play elevates him to legendary status.

Play Ball!
Bob "Steady" Simmons was the Royal Ace

In the modern era, one might wrongly assume that hitting a softball is inherently easier than knocking a hard-ball out of the park. But anyone familiar with windmill-pitched softball knows better, especially when an ace pitcher is on the mound and in command of a high-speed sinker. Blink, and you miss.

Such a pitcher, playing a pivotal role in the 1957 Twilight League Season, was Bobby Simmons of the Royals.

Simmons performance on the mound had a bit in common with a now relatively obscure Big Leaguer named Jack Sanford of the Phillies who was named National League Rookie of the Year just 12 months earlier A hard-throwing righty, Sanford would manage a season record of 19-7, leading the National League in strikeouts.

One sportswriter characterized Sanford in this way: "He would not be a Cadillac, but he was a damn good Buick."

That was also a pretty good description of the fast-pitch Royals' ace thrower Bobby Simmons. His stuff was not overwhelming. Yet he commanded respect with an-above average fastball, curve, and sinker -- plus he offered a "positive presence" when he took the mound. Bob "Steady" Simmons was always ready for a challenge. He had long been the mainstay of the Royals' pitching staff (along with Bill Marino) and was counted on to bring his team the championship in 1957.

Laying in wait were several menacing rivals, the most threatening being the Tectapers. The early games that season would underscore the importance of pitching power. The first real confrontation of powerhouses took place on June 15 between the Royals and Tectape. Fans anticipated the match up as an indicator of any changes in the balance of power in the league. These teams dominated the scene in previous years.

The showdown got off to a rousing beginning. Versatile Dan Brandon, himself a pitcher, hit a homer with two on base in the first inning. With the score 3 to 0 at the top of the third, the Royals scored when Stroman doubled and scored on Bruce Flowers single.

That score held as Tech's Brandon bested the Royal's Bobby Simmons with a final tally of 3 to 1.

Early Season Contests
A Memorable Brandon-Piedmont Pitching Duel

57

Other early games that season also underscore the importance of pitching. A good example comes from Dave Mullony who pitched his team the HiLiters to a win over the Adlers. In other action, the Bonefoy Club whacked the Whirls - 9 to 1 - with Buddy Fay holding the Whirls to a single run. That win was supported by a Bonefro batting offense by Dom Scazzero, Vin Connelly, and Bill Renire.

In the Industrial League, opponents squared off. Notable was John Mandarano who had the hot bat that spring, bringing the Rogues to early contention.

Batters also got their due. Box scores printed in the the Standard Star newspaper heralded game-winning hits in early-season play. An example: Two hitters from the TMC team, Vic Gibson and John Serena were noted as contributing to victories over the rival Gries.

Meanwhile, Frost Men's Shop got off to a good start by toppling Founders behind the bats of Mike Immediato and Dom Bucello.

The Fort Slocum team known then as the "Squirrels" kept up a torrid pace of early wins.

In early June there were several key games within each division. The American Legion Post-8 rode an offense provided by shortstop Frank Miceli and Carlo Catalanotto to beat the Castoffs, 4 to 3.

The Popeye Nine triumphed over Gay Dome, sparked by George Gallo and Charles Rigano, each supplying a duo of game-deciding hits. It was the Popeyes' Pat Dorme who registered the pitching win.

In the middle of the first round, the Popeyes upended the Frosts, 5 to 4, to stay unbeaten. Mickey Circelli's two-out single provided the winning margin.

One of the most memorable contests in 1957 occurred in June at City Park. A pitching match up pitted Dan Brandon against Lou Piedmont of the Bonnies.

It was a windmill version of Harvey Haddix's major league achievement for the Pittsburgh Pirates. For those who don't remember: Haddix "lost" the game despite giving up no hits in extra innings.

In this case, it was Len Piedmont who pitched a no hitter against one of the best batting lineups in the league. He did it over eight innings. Brandon threw a three hitter. Yet the score wound up an inconclusive 0 to 0. Stalemate!

Rogues Threaten Boycott!!!

News coverage offers limelight for star players

57

Following his duel with Len Piedmont, Brandon extended his shutout string to 19 innings with a blanking of the Blue Birds.

Around mid-June, the "Paris" Rogues stifled the Royals (this year called the Tropical Casino Royals due to sponsorship) with an outstanding performance by Lefty Ianuzzi of the Rogues.

The Rogues were looking for a win. But then threatened to boycott play to protest an umpire's decision.

The game finally went on with the Rogues getting hits by Cookie Norberto and Tut Mandarano followed by a round-tripper by Ianuzzi. Although they battled back, the Royals fell short with their second defeat in the second-round of play.

Boycotts and fighting with umpires was not typical in the Twilight Era. A young man's temper might flare, but being "sportsmanlike" was an idea affixed in a player's mind and encouraged by coaches.

Still, local sports had its brawls. And an unusual incident occurred later that summer which potentially could have adversely affected fast-pitch softball. A player for the New Rochelle Robins, a semi-pro team in the Westchester Colonial League, assaulted an umpire. Afterwards, a meeting was arranged consisting of umpires, city officials, team reps, and the general public.

All agreed to a "grievance procedure" which was later used in cases involving raucous conduct on the diamond. The official message was clear: baseball must never be mixed with boxing between innings. And it rarely was.

There was little reason to fight, anyway. Players came to compete. And those who did well found themselves stars of the lowest wattage due to ample coverage in the newspaper during this period.

The local paper, the Standard Star let softball fans know about upcoming matchups. And this reporting kindled serious interest. Whenever Piedmont, Brandon or Simmons pitched, a crowd was sure to be there.

Status followed league success. And one of the brightest spots in the Senior League American Division in 1957 was the steady pitching of Len Piedmont. The newspaper noted that after hurling a no-hitter, Piedmont followed with a three-hit whitewashing of the Calabria club. Len was now in the limelight.

Second Round, Upsets Galore!
Paris Rogues Slide into First Place

57

Second-round upsets continued. The third-place Paris Rogues were toppled by Strobl's behind Jim Stone's steady pitching and timely slugging from Joe Mercurio.

So after the Rogues beat the Royals, they in turn got trapped by Strobl's. Stone held a no hitter for the Rogues for six and two-third innings before Cookie Norberto knocked a 2-2 pitch into right center at Isaac Young Field for a home run. At that time, only Tectape remained unbeaten in season play. And the Royals' Bobby Simmons was peaking with consecutive wins.

The Royals had easily won the first round of the Twilight League play. And after a shaky second round start, they hit their stride. The turning point came on Bill Marino's masterful five-hitter in a victory over Bonefro. Bill Dorkim's home run for the Bonnies was the only run surrendered by the Royals. Chauncey Williams, Al Richardson, and Cliff Shelton made up the winning offense for the Royals.

Meanwhile in the National Division, the Popeyes took the league lead with a drubbing of Calabria, 9 to 1, with multiple hit performances by John DeMasi, George Gallo and Tony Giordano as the spinach men built a solid lead.

During the next week, in June's sweltering heat, another classic duel in the sun took place between Simmons and Brandon, two of the best in the league. It was similar to the battle going on in the Major League baseball: the statistical tug-of-war between Mickey Mantle and Ted Williams.

On July 5th, Mantle held a lead over Williams in batting average .388 to .349. For home runs, it was 22 for Mantle and 20 for Williams. Comparing RBIs, it was 55 for Mantle and 50 for Williams. (Roy Sievers had 54 RBIs but without a leading batting average to go with it.)

The headline in the Standard Star read "It's anyone's race as Bonnies upset Tectapes." Bonefro became the latest team to pull an upset in the American Division by dousing Tectape 5 to 2, and -- in doing so -- pinned a loss on Brandon. Al Ryder homered for the Tapers in the loss. As a result, the Paris Rogues climbed to first place as Bonefro tied Techtape for the second-place slot.

POPEYE NINE

The Spinach Men Rise to the Top

57

By the second round of play, the different divisions were tightening up in the standings. The Fort Slocum Squirrels were clearly ahead in the Industrial division, Frost Men's' Shop was unbeaten in the National Division with the Forresters and Popeyes close behind. The Frosts were paced by Dom Bucello and Butch Hendrie along with pitchers Sal Caporale and Don Chadric.

In the Senior Division, the Rogues also were once-beaten and held a slim lead over Tectape and Strobl's. The Royals, with two losses, slipped to fifth place behind the Bonnies.

Down the stretch, every game was key.

Simmons three-hitter against the Rogues prompted the Royals move to the league summit. It was shaping up to be an interesting month of August. This was especially true of the Popeye Nine. The Popeyes rode the crest of 20-game win streak.

The Popeye's streak of victories reached 21 games with a win over Gay Dome, 6 to 0. Once again it was Pat Dorme, this time tossing a three-hitter.

That game had been delayed due to a car crash at Washington and Seventh Street involving a 1956 Plymouth convertible and a 1954 Ford Crestline.

Still, luck was with the Popeyes now on target to clinch the National Division.

The Popeye Nine featured some of the youngest players in the Twilight League. It was a relative newcomer in a field of well established clubs. Still, coach Anthony "Popeye" Claps who ran a stationery store on Union Avenue saw his team rise to prominence on what might be described as a miraculous win streak. Apparently, the Popeye players ate their spinach in 1957.

The Popeyes position lineup for the clincher:

1b-Rigano
2b-Pisani
3b DeMasi
ss-Sabia
lf-Semenza
cf-Letizia
rf-Giordano
P-Dorme
C-Gallo

The Popeyes went an amazing 21 games undefeated

Guns of August
Fans Abuzz about Season Closers

In early August, slugger Cookie Norberto struck again, this time breaking pitcher Dan Brandon's amazing 28-scoreless-innings mark as the Tapers beat the Paris Rogues, 7 to 1.

Billy Bohn's hitting paced the Tectapes with a 3-for-3 day.

Meanwhile, in the National Division, the Forresters kept the Popeye Niners from winning the division. It was a tie game, 1 to 1. At bat, Jim Sabia and George Gallo garnered two hits apiece for the championship-seeking Popeyes.

It was getting deeper into August which meant it was crunch time –the playoffs had arrived. In a year of surprises, the first series to be decided was the Industrial Division. Sure enough there was an upset.

Attendance at Playoff Games was Measured in the Thousands...

The Fort Slocum Squirrels were crushed by Adler's in two straight games. After defeating Fort Slocum in the first playoff game, 5 to 2, Tony Rascona of the Adlers went 5 for 5. Combined with John Riley's timely hitting, stole the Slocum Squirrels' last nuts. The winning pitcher was Rascona.

Next on tap was the dramatic showdown between Tectape and Royals. The Royals manager Will Richardson squared off against Techtape's Mario Perri. Bill Marino toed the rubber for the Royals and Dan Brandon stood on the mound for the Tapers. Both lineups included a bevy of great batters. For the Royals, it was Stroman, Shelton, Richardson and three Flowers brothers. For Tectape, it was Bohn, Ryder, Robinson and Lybrand.

By this stage of the season, interest bolstered by daily sports page coverage was huge. A crowd estimated at 2,000 packed City Park to see Cliff "Jabbo" Shelton escape the tag in a rundown and give the Royals a lead they never relinquished.

Bill Marino bested Danny Brandon with an assist from Bobby Simmons in relief. Game Two saw Tectape seize advantage of the Royals' pitchers sudden wildness to win the contest, 6 to 5, the difference being Bruce Flowers walking Al Ryder with the bases full. Game Three would decide who would advance.

The Edge of Victory

It was as if New Rochelle had its own Subway Series

New Rochelle was abuzz. The opening series had the Royals edging Brandon, 1 to 0. Later it was Tectape who responded with their own 6 to 5 victory. Game Three ended 1 to 1. It just couldn't get any closer, and standing in the wings were the Popeye Nine with an unblemished record of 22 to 0.

Sports editor Bob Hrgoesch of the Standard Star called the upcoming final game between the two clubs "one of the most exciting softball races in the history of New Rochelle."

Previous games attracted upwards of 3,000 fans and a larger crowd was anticipated for the final game with Tectape. Records suggest attendance grew by a third in the latter playoffs, as coverage in papers invited more speculation about who would be champion.

Hardly anyone attended the movies that Friday evening. It was now Twilight Time.

A bustling city in 1957, with a downtown that was - on the high-end - the Beverly Hills of its day, New Rochelle could hardly be called Middle America. Yet, here was a town that avidly embraced its fast-pitch league as if it were home to multiple minor league teams facing each other in a subway series. In post season play, crowds that represented almost 5 percent of the city's population gathered. It was like having fireworks every night for two weeks and no one tired of coming, watching and cheering.

It was Friday August 23, 1957. Game time was set at 5:30 p.m. At RKO Proctors on Main Street "Night Passage," starring James Stewart and Audie Murphy was playing. At Loews, it was "Young Don't Cry" with Sal Mineo and James Whitemore. At Pelham, "Island in the Sun" played.

Hardly anyone attended the movies that Friday evening. It was now twilight time.

With Tectape first baseman Chico Ramos out of the lineup on injury, coach Mario Perri relied on rotating two outfielders at first base. This slight advantage was key to the Royals winning, 4 to 3. A miscue by a replacement player at first base during the top of the seventh was all the Royals needed to eliminate Tectape. Stroman drove in the winning run - a frequent occurrence that summer. Simmons was the winning pitcher. A Royal-Popeye finale loomed.

Royal-Popeye Finale
Standing Room Only as Fans Flooded Fields

57

So it would be the reigning Royals against an unbeaten Popeye Nine for the city title.

The Impending Finale Would Draw 3,000 Spectators to a New Rochelle Ball Field for a Single Game. Some 15,000 Fans Would Attend the Playoffs as a Series, a Level Simply Staggering by Modern Standards.

The Royals series with Tectape was as close as one could imagine. Now it was Pat Dorme and Phil Mercurio's turn to battle the Royals in a best of three for the city crown. The championship series would start the next day, Saturday.

With a 22-game unbeaten streak at stake, Pat Dorme took the mound for Popeye's with Bill Marino toiling for the Royals. Each team managed only three hits- Popeye's (Gallo 2, Bongo 1) Royals (Williams 1, Kemp 1, and Duarte 1).

The playoff for the city championship began. Wives complained they had not seen their husbands for the five straight days of playoff games. The margin of victory, one run, was provided by Jabbo Shelton's alert base running. This was the Royals' calling card: always take care of the little things which will add up to victories- and - stay balanced between defense and offense. The Royals had scored one run in the top of the first when Shelton led off the game with a bunt that the Popeye first baseman didn't cleanly handle.Shelton then stole second and scored on a throwing error. The play of the day however was turned in by Will Richardson, player-manager of the Royals who robbed Ron Semenza of a home run by making a leaping catch of his second-inning blast. Final score: Royals 1, Popeyes 0.

It's hard to explain how exciting this all was for 15,000 fans attending these final games of the 1957 Season.

A Stunning 315-Foot Homer at Morgan Field

Of special note, history was made at New Rochelle's Morgan Field when Jim Garrison had one of the most extraordinary days in New York sports. Playing for the Bears Little League team on June 14, Garrison crushed one homer a major-league distance of 315 feet. And to top that off, he knocked three more out of the park. Quite a feat!

Royals Rally Against Popeyes
Fast-Pitch Hits its Apogee in Momentous Final

57

Game Two of the Royals-Popeyes Series was yet another classic. With both squads exhibiting championship flair, the Popeyes held a precarious lead in the second game - 2 to 1 - by the late innings. The Royals were in serious trouble. One more out would catapult the Popeye Nine to its first playoff win.

But Charlie Billups of the Royals sliced a hit to left, off Mercurio. Simmons drew a walk and with two on, one out. Anthony "Popeye" Claps strolled out to the mound and quietly asked "Philly Merc" for the ball. Popeye had few options at this point and calls for the reliable arm of Pat Dorme.

Next, Shelton popped up and it was two outs. Popeye fans cheered every pitch. Kemp is the next up and he digs in at the back of the batters box with his bat elevated over his head. He rakes Dorme's first pitch past shortstop Jim Sabia and ties the game.

The third out is made when Simmons is caught in a rundown. The momentum shifts. In extra innings, the Royals wasted no time: Stroman singles, then Flowers does the same.

Right fielder Rocky Orsini took Flowers single and fired the ball to second base where it took an odd bounce and drifted to left field. Turner Stroman who had advanced to third heeded his coach's directions to go keep going and scampered to touch home.

The Royals had found a way to win. Pitchers Simmons and Marino got the win. The Royals prevailed.

Even in defeat, the Popeye Nine gave a good account of themselves. They played well and managed a lossless regular season. And there would be 1958...

The big winners were the fans. Between 15,000 to 18,000 people were thrilled with unbelievably close games. Fast-pitch reached its apogee in 1957 thanks to these nail-biting showdowns in the Twilight League.

Wives Complained they had not seen their husbands for the five straight days of the playoffs...

The Real Popeye

Coach Anthony Claps Summons Roy Rogers to Town

When Anthony 'Popeye' Claps promised local kids in New Rochelle that he would bring cowboy singer Roy Rogers to town for a visit, few believed him. Little did they know Clap's brother Danny had been an entertainer who worked with Rogers in the past. Soon enough the famed cowboy arrived on horseback on Union Avenue, one day in the late 1940s with his entire troupe and Trigger. Popeye 'stories' usually proved true.

Claps was called "Popeye" by his younger friends because of his bulgy forearms. And he was a 'character' in his own right. The Claps clan of many brothers and sisters was one of the best known families from "Up the West."

A coach and sponsor of the Popeye Nine, Claps could be proud of his young ball club in 1957. They had made it through the regular season undefeated -- and after 20 consecutive wins, victories were hard to count.

It was now the off-season. For the softball coaches, the real problem was keeping the same players together for a "next" year. For "Popeye" Anthony Claps, it was a return full time to his stationery store on the corner of of Union and Fifth. For Claps,

there would be plenty to talk about until the next season.

After 20 Consecutive Wins, Popeye had Trouble Keeping Track of Victories in 1957

His young ball club proved to be a class act and came, oh-so close, to grabbing the brass ring in 1957.

Popeye and those who frequented his store for cigarettes, candy and soda loved to engage in the art of ego deflation or the "putdown" usually poking fun at someone or something.

Telling jokes with his infectious laugh was part of the routine, not to mention argument for argument's sake, usually over who was better Mickey, Willie or the Duke.

Popeye could take solace in that his nucleus players would return next season: Dorme, Mercurio, Sabia, Giordano, Gallo, and Telesco. 1958! It would prove an interesting year, again, for the Popeye Nine.

HALL OF FAME

Fearless Frisch

An occasional visitor to softball and Little League games at City Park was New Rochelle resident and baseball Hall of Famer Frankie Frisch. Frisch during the 1950's was an announcer on a post game show for New York Giants games. He had been a versatile all American football player at Fordham University and carried that versatility to baseball when he concentrated on becoming a switch hitter utilizing his unusual speed to compile a .316 lifetime average. A member of the Gas House Gang on St Louis, Frisch had been traded from the Giants to the Cards for Rogers Hornsby. In an interview with WFAS Radio, Frisch said the young ballplayer should be fearless; if they can't reach their goals keep trying. The important thing, he said was for players to devote their time to develop skills and be the best you can— a thought we must always keep in the forefront

Moore Field at Isaac Young

Pictured on the left is the original location of Moore Field, which was relocated to another spot at the same site. Also missing are wooden stands where fans could watch Twilight League play in the 1950s. Note, the vast width of the field posed challenges to outfielders.

City Park Field

City Park was the home of base of the Twilight League where championships would be played. Pictured is the old administration office of the New Rochelle Department of Recreation. It is known as Brud Flowers Field, in dedication to a member of the fast-pitch Royals.

CARL D'ONOFRIO
1916 - 2009
LITTLE LEAGUE:
FIRST COACH
FIRST UMPIRE
FIRST IN OUR HEART

D'Onofrio Field, located in the city's southside, looks today more or less like it did when established in the 1950s. The sports park is named after members of New Rochelle's D'Onofrio family. Pictured (above) is a plaque to Carl D'Onofrio who was very active in promoting and supporting local youth sports and is fondly remembered with this memorial. Pictured below is a view of home plate from the pitcher's mound

Columbus Field

Located in the West End of New Rochelle at the Columbus elementary school was one of the fields used by the Twilight League. Pictured here is the location of the original center and right fields (right being near the white fence.) The field was later moved a short distance, placing it closer to Feeney Park and aside the Mascaro Branch of the Boys Club (not pictured and off to the left.)

1958

Fast-Pitches

TV Ate My Kids:

Outside the chalk lines of the ball field, the song Purple People Eater rocketed to Number One on charts while the inane Gigi was voted best picture over Cat on a Hot Tin Roof. Parents complained kids watched too much television. Pope Pius XII declared Claire of Assisi patron saint of TV. Not everyone was watching the tube, though. Horse tracks at Yonkers and Roosevelt were averaging about 25,000 people a night without the benefits of exotic wagering - no exactas or trifectas.

Rookie of the Year

It was the year a rookie outfielder from the state of North Dakota would begin a pro career. Later, his home run assault in 1961 for the New York Yankees would surprise an unsuspecting baseball world as he challenged and eventually broke one of the game's most sacred records.

The player was Roger Maris who arrived at the Cleveland Indians in 1958. Maris later sent shockwaves through the major leagues when he eclipsed the single-season record of 60 homers held by Babe Ruth.

THE NUMBERS

The daily "numbers" or "Policy Numbers" were the illegal precursor of our current state lottery. Bettors typically paid five or ten cents on the chance to win $50 for guessing on the "straight number." Some bet on the first or third digit of the number for a lesser payoff. On a typical day people would stick their head in stores and ask about the number or the "drop" digit (the last digit). One day, an unsuspecting visitor from the Midwest inquired why so many people were asking about these "numbers." The New Rochelle store owner quickly responded it was the street address for someone in the neighborhood. The visitor shrugged and left.

Street Corner Music

A Capella

Over the byways of history, there have appeared those who freelanced their musical talents: minstrels and troubadours. These talents graced our avenues with evocative song and dance. The fifties, too, produced street-corner talent. Among New Rochelle's best known "A capella" singers were Louie Nardone and Frank Claps. While other towns had their own 50s-style serenaders, few had folks like Claps who had the rare opportunity to sing with Chuck Berry during a summer block party at Columbus School. Clap's on-stage version of "Rock Around the Clock" saw teens dancing into the night.

During those Rock-N-Roll inspired days of Chuck Berry, local a-cappella groups made music of their own, using Feeney Park as their "open-air recording studio." They sang tunes again and again until they got the "right" sound they sought. A rare few later received recording contracts, but most were happy enough just entertaining themselves -- and all within earshot -- on hot summer nights in Westchester and the Bronx.

A Race to the Summit
Players at their Peak Plan a Prodigious Push

58

The world of fast-pitch softball in New Rochelle had hit a peak of sorts the previous year. A certain level of maturity was apparent with the opening of the 1958 Season. A volume of good players proliferated in the Twilight League. Veteran players who inspired these new entrants to fast-pitch play were themselves at their personal summit of experience and skill.

The city champs, the Royals saw its dynasty players getting on in years. Yet, they remained solid favorites for a repeat run at the title.

The season ushered in a particularly formidable group of teams ready to topple the blue-clad family of Royals. And by a quirk of fate, one would.

Contenders were the Adlers, TMC, Bonefro Club, Forresters, and Popeye Nine.

Again, there was Tectape. Under Mario Perri's leadership the Tectapers had in the past come within one play of winning the title for a first time.

The race for to reach the summit began in earnest....

NO LEEWAY!

With the start of the season, Fred Todora and his staff at the City Recreation Office did their typical great job making sure baseball diamonds were ready for the season's start.

Bert Terranova and Nello Amori played key roles in keeping the grounds ready for ball especially when inclement weather required special attention. Infields had to be raked and chalk lines drawn for the foul lines and batters box. A wooden template was used for the batters box and bases. More dramatically, rain soaked fields would be lit aflame and burned with oil to speed up drying.

Mimeographed green-colored sheets were handed out for players to ascertain the time, place and field number for games. "There shall be no leeway" was printed at the end of each sheet as a sort of an official stamp of authority.

Tectape's Secret Weapon

Forresters convincingly clinch

58

Sterling pitching performances highlighted the opening week of the season. In a stunner, the Popeye Nine upset the defending champion Royals, 6 to 1, behind hurler Phil Mercurio's one hitter. Then Donald Summo's two-hit gem carried the Bonnies over the Whirls.

Next, Lee Hollis of Tectape threw a no hitter against the Frosts. This pitching prowess by Hollis proved a new weapon for Tectape. The team already had one of the best arms in the league- that of Dan Brandon. Now it had two cannons on call.

Yet it wasn't all about pitchers that second week in May. George Rituno scored three times and provided two extra base hits for the victorious Gems. Other offensive bursts -- from Ernie Reiehl, Charlie Rigano and Mike Merigliano -- propelled an assortment of early season wins.

Fans were surprised by the closeness of the race for the championship. Younger teams had taken finally found a way to put a dent in the veteran Royals and Tectape. It would be a contest in 1958, and the contenders would take no prisoners. A series of blowouts commenced.

The Forresters were sure their time had come. Behind veteran hurler, Ed Efferin, they clinched the National Division crushing the Nomads, 19 to 1. Key players for the Forresters during the season were Mike Merigliano, Woody Woodell, George Pierro and Efferin.

Edging closer to the American Division title, the Popeye Nine blasted the Whirls, 18 to 0, with Sherman Downer and Billy Telesco providing the firepower.

The Industrial Division championship game took place at Isaac Young Field. With pitcher George Mittlestadt leading the way by allowing only four hits, the Splicers routed TMC, 10 to 0. Tom Meola provided an offensive punch, going 3 for 4.

At Columbus Field, Phil Mercurio posted his fifth shutout of the season blanking the Frosts, 2 to 0. The win moved Popeyes a game ahead of Tectape -- and ahead of the Royals -- in the American Division. Shortstop John DeMasi's key defensive stops and Billy Telesco's long ball sparked the Popeyes.

Tectape's Revenge
Tenacious Tapers take title

58

Finally, a championship match was set: Tectape versus the Forresters. The Tapers had survived the summer competition from the Royals, Popeyes and Bonnefoy Club to emerge in the finals. The longshot Forresters, backed by the experienced arms of Efferen and Woodell, were hopeful the year of upsets would continue.

> **The Techsters wasted no time, scoring seven times**

In the championship series for the New Rochelle title it was the best of three games. Amidst the threat of showers during that summer weekend at City Park, right-hander Dan Brandon, a bit weary from endlessinnings pitched during the season, took to the mound for the American title while Eddie Efferen toed the rubber for the Forresters. The Techsters wasted no time,scoring seven times in a second frame to vanquish the Forresters. A combined tandem of Brandon and Lee Hollis held their opponent to three hits. Paced by Sonny Robinson's three run homer, Tectape took the opener, 8 to 1. In the second game, the next day, right-hander Hollis opposed 54-year-old "Woody" Woodell of the Forresters. In the first inning, the Tapers scored all the runs they needed, managing to tally four. Amazingly, theTapers scored all four runs on only one hit. Final score: Tectape 4, Forresters 1.

So the curtain closed on 1958 - a year full of surprises, disappointments, and retribution. The tenacious Tectapers and their strong-willed manager Mario Perri had reached the mountaintop. Several teams couldn't wait until the spring of 1959 to knock them off that summit.

```
Championship
Lineup for
TecTape
1B- Ryder
2B- Meade
SS- Robinson
3B- Becker
LF- Bahn
Cf- Archer
RF- Esposito
C-  Lybrand
P - Brandon
```

Tectape wasted no time, scoring seven times

End of Fast-Pitch as We Know It?

A more mass-participant sports threatens windmill

Fast-Pitch softball had reached its apex in the late 1950s. Why? It's important to remember that this pitching-led game of skill first attracted adherents in the late 1930s and early 40s who then formed local leagues across the country. The Twilight League of New Rochelle in the 1950s represented players who were the sport's second-generation participants. And fast-pitch had its downside. For starters, the game relied on pitching wizards who were a rare breed and couldn't be mass produced. As a result, it was a hard sport to keep balanced as the best pitching clubs would chronically crush the competition in blowouts.

Fast-pitch was a serious sport where rare talent was a must at the mound. It also fell under the umbrella of local recreation, and towns were looking for a friendlier version that would allow more participation from a wider "mass" audience.

The answer was "slow-pitch." During midsummer in Armonk, the town's recreation department sponsored a 22-team slow-pitch tournament involving players from the region. It marked one of the largest ever contests for the slow-pitch variety of softball in that era. From here on, this new version would grow tremendously and spread throughout the tristate area - eventually replacing its fast-pitch predecessor.

Fast-pitch would thrive for another few years in places like New Rochelle. But its Twilight League devotees of the 1950s would soon seem like Don Quixote's ageing squires, cherishing memories of chasing windmills. Eventually, windmill would end entirely. Potential players chose either hardball or the new slow-pitch variety of softball as their game of choice. Only a women's version of the sport would continue to prosper locally, bolstered by a growing number of college scholarship opportunities.

The story of windmill would continue into the 1960s. But there could be little doubt the term Twilight League took on a double meaning as the 1950s headed for a close. This amazing chapter in sports history rushed to a conclusion. There were still surprises and plenty of riveting box scores ahead.

Twilight approached

Era's Greats Gather to Duel

Slow-pitch softball was just too slow for Roy Stevenson, the bullet-throwing Softball Hall of Famer who had helped the windmill-style version of the sport first win acclaim in the 40s.

Born in Hicksville, Long Island, Roy's initial fame came from years playing for Grumann Aerospace, who later built the lunar lander. He was declared an All American in 1948, 1950, 1958 and 1959. Honored as he was, Stevenson was still probably underrated. Consider this: Playing for the Shamrocks of New Rochelle in 1938, he once struck out an incredible 28 batters in a row in West Haven, Conn.

Now, the star of 1940s windmill play was getting his due. In 1958, a fast-pitch tournament was held in his honor in Mount Vernon, gathering the region's top players.

The August tournament was a "who is s who" of the sport for the 1950s. The list of players who signed up to participate was unlike anything New York had ever seen.

When the dust settled, the title game matched the Mount Vernon Standards against the New Rochelle Tectapes. Pitching duties were assumed by Walt Helfer and Frank Paul.

Helfer was on the money tossing a two hitter up until the sixth inning's third batter. Too bad he was up against the peerless pitching of Rush Riley.

After Rich Surhoff replaced Paul on the mound for Tectape, the Standards broke the ice with a squeeze play by Paul Vecchione.

That was all Rush needed to cement the win, 2 to 0.

A crowd of 500 buzzed about the great confrontations they witnessed at the tournament, which featured its namesake, Stevenson, joining in the play.

There was much to discuss. A controversy reverberated throughout the county in the wake of this great showdown. The sports editor of the local newspaper, the Standard Star, Bob Hrubesch, fired the first volley by accusing the manager of Tectape, Mario Perri of withholding one of his ace pitchers Dick Surhoff in a game against a county league opponent. Perri was accused of not going "all out" to win. True or not, it was a bold declaration considering how seriously Perri was known to take his coaching.

Hrubesch was begging for a rebuttal. One soon followed.

CONTROVERSY ERUPTS!

```
MOUNT VERNON                 NEW ROCHELLE ROYALS
STANDARDS
                             William Richardson
Donald "Rush" Riley          Turner Stroman
Tony Veteri                  Ed Green
Babe Gabbamonte              Cookie Norberto


MOUNT VERNON                 NEW ROCHELLE TECTAPE
SUNDOWNERS
                             Sonny Robinson
Peanuts Leriness             Mario Perri (coach)
Jack Henning                 Frank Paul
Bernie Tanzillo
Bob Lapple


MAMARONECK EAGLES            EASTCHESTER GO-GOs

Norm McClendon               Horace Banks


WHITE PLAINS T-BIRDS         YONKERS GOLIO OLYMPIANS

Steve Clowe                  Richard Bork


LEVITTOWN MEENAN OILERS

Roy Stevenson
```

Surhoff had indicated to a reporter he was ready to pitch. Perri responded to the column with his own published letter documenting his long coaching resume. Sentiment ran both for Perri and against him.

For all the distractions created by the controversy, Perri would have the last laugh.

Here's what occurred:

The Royals started the third inning of the county league game with consecutive singles by Simmons and Shelton. With the Royals already ahead, 1-0, it behooved Perri to bring in his ace, Surhoff. Perri opted to stay with the overworked Brandon who was touched for five straight.

His Tectape team won the Twilight League title for 1958. If he was initially miffed by Hrubesch's sporting remarks, he would soon rest on the laurels of a hard won of a season victory.

1959

Fast Pitches

End of an Era

Russian Race to Space

A Russian moon rocket launched in 1959 was timed to match Nikita Krushchev's trip to the States. As he prepared for a summit meeting in the U.S. with top officials, the Russian Space Agency announced lunar mission was attempting to map an area around the moon. Russian rocketry was increasingly linked to global propaganda efforts. A U.S. lunar landing was still a decade in the future. For now, it was the early days of Project Mercury. Americans were still playing catch up to their Soviet rivals in the race to explore space.

Schult Joins the Cubs

Arthur "Dutch" Schult became Westchester's sole Major Leaguer when the Chicago Cubs signed a contract for the White Plains resident in 1959.

The right-handed Schult reported to the Cubs and doubled in his first at bat, driving in base runner Ernie Banks. Schult's career stats were .264 with six homers and 56 RBIs.

He wasn't new to the majors. Schult had been a Red Sox and later joined the Yankees. But before signing with Chicago, he had set up residence in White Plains.

SLOW-PITCH ARRIVES

A telling headline in the May 30 Edition of the Standard Star was in a quiet way a sign of the future: "Slow Pitch Debut Set." The article goes on to to say a game will be played on Monday between Pelham Produce and Mayflower Café. The popularity of slow pitch was gaining momentum.

WRESTLING IN WHITE PLAINS

The County Center hosted wrestling with the Graham Brothers against Dan Curtis and Mark Lee. A thousand fans also watched Little Chief Big Heart defeat Honest Harry and his Mexican Jumping Bean partner, Pepe Charcharro. In single matches, Baron Van Hess was upset by Miguel Torres. Mighty Jumbo whipped Tony Martelli.

End of An Era - Almost

Old sports never die. They just fade a bit...

59

Everything Changes...

Times change. Names fade. Eras end. Things return. And history is full of surprises that can shape how we think about the present and the future - even sports history.

Consider that the New Rochelle Handicap horse race that first ran back in 1899 at the Morris Park Racecourse in Westchester County, New York. It switched to Belmont Park in 1904 when Morris Park closed, and the site - geographically - was no longer part of the county. It was annexed by the Bronx. However, the New Rochelle Handicap continued at Belmont, on and off, until 1918 when it was resurrected at Empire City in Yonkers. That year, the Preakness Stakes winner War Cloud also won the New Rochelle Handicap. Once again, the race was moved -- to Jamaica Racetrack in Queens in 1943, which later closed in August 1959.The New Rochelle name likely continued in the race's title because it added a sense of gentility to the affair that - in its earliest days - served as a local version of the Kentucky Derby with robber-barons lookalikes and women in oversized hats crowding stands. The archaic name persisted, as did the race. But as eras lapsed, meanings and associations changed.

Much of that was true for the fast-pitch softball era of the 1950s. Windmill didn't start that decade, nor did it end. But it was the sport's golden age, based on its prevalence, the size of its following and arguably it over-sized pool of talent. And 1959 was the final year of fast-pitch's most successful decade. And it was the start of its descent.

There are similarities between the decline of thoroughbred horse racing and fast-pitch softball. Social and cultural changes, and the advent of increased media -- radio and then television programming -- changed the world upon which ballfields and tracks were built.

New activities don't eliminate the basic games. Old sports never die. They just fade a bit. Or in some cases, they find a new form as in racing which found off-track wagering, and fast-pitch softball which found its ways into the hands of an almost exclusively female clientele who traded 1900s race-track bonnets for 1980s b-ball caps. Who can say which developments are the most surprising in the end?

The Great Exhibition of 1959

Roy Stephenson's win record was 28 to 4 at the time

Charity Play

The Summer of 1959 saw one of the most successful windmill pitchers make an all star appearance in New Rochelle. Roy Stevenson and his team called DuJour took on Sound Shore all stars at Columbus Field in a benefit game. Participants were New Rochelle's Goo Goo Green, Sonny Robinson, Turner Stroman Horace Lybrand, Sal Sclafani, Billy Telesco, DickMeade, Nick Samela, and Ed Sharkey. Mario Perri coached. The umpires were Joe Piedmont, Ernie Motta, Gene Salazzo, James Tiernan, and Lou Semenza

Roy Stephenson's win record was 28-4 at the time. The charity game turned out to be thriller with 1,700 windmill-softball faithful packed into a crowded Columbus School Field to watch the New Rochelle All Stars lose an exciting 13-inning contest to DuJour led by Stephenson. In fact, Stephenson struck out a total of 16 after New Rochelle took an initial lead of 2 to 1. The All Stars scored on a hit by Lybrand, a bunt single by Bill Telesco, and sac fly by DiBuono.

Unfinished Business for Royals

The season came with an automatic exclamation mark attached

59

The final year of the decade brought intrinsic drama. Change was coming and everyone felt a hyperbolic pinch that whatever happened next would be the last time it would for the "Fab 50s."

On that note, the 1959 Twilight League Season came with an automatic exclamation mark attached. Some foresaw a season of reckoning.

The Royals felt it. They had unfinished business to care for as the 1959 season opned. In 1958, they lost their first Twilight title in over ten years, to Tectape.

Tectaper's coach Mario Perri, of course, felt his team was destined to do it again without any drastic changes in strategy. He believed "Tec" had the edge and had last year's trophy to prove it.

Other teams were more practical in prepping. In an effort to boost offense, the Popeye Nine added several new players. This was out of necessity. A number of key personnel had defected to the Frost's Men Shop team and Popeye refused to change his squad's name to the Popeye Four.

Either way, the Popeyes were untested. And in first round action, the Royals, took first place in the American division by routing an the Popeye Niners. The Royals Turner Stroman and Jabbo Shelton garnered 3 hits for the lopsided win.

Meanwhile, over at Columbus Field, ex-Popeyers Pat Dorme of Frosts pitched a two hitter against the Forresters. Mike Immediato and Tony Giordano got key hits for the winners.

The reigning Tectape champs were looking strong with Danny Brandon fashioning a four hitter against Strobl's. Of note, shortstop Sonny Robinson of Tectape stroked three hits, distinguishing himself as one of the league's best all-around players.

In the National Division, the Gems stopped the Whirls, 5 to 4, annexing first place utilizing three clutch hits from batters Cliff O'Dell, Don Gibson, and Ken Necerato.

First round play continued with the high note being Philly Merurio's masterful two hitter against Tectape, 1 to 0, giving the Popeye's a rebound win.

Champs or not, Tectape's aura of invincibility disappeared.

Deadlocked for First
Royals and Tectape Come to Swings

59

Tectape deadlocked the Royals for first place by beating Frost's Mens Shop, 5 to 1. Pitcher Danny Brandon held Frosts to five hits while he received run support from Funicello and Lybrand. Sal Caporale took the loss for Frosts.

Things then turned red hot in the senior softball league when the Tapers beat Blue Birds, 8 to 1, and Frost's tied the Royals - 8 to 8 - on Mike Immediato's homer. In the former, Sonny Robinson continued his hot Streak for Tectape. While in the latter, Dan Dwarte's grandslam for the Royals kept them close to first place.

In the first round of the National Division, Tani's was coasting 8 to 2 over the Gems when suddenly the Gems scored 11 runs in the fifth frame to beat Tani's. Gabe Carino was the winning pitcher for the Gems and Carlo Catalanotto lost it for Tani's.

The Tani's bounced back in their next game to whitewash the FireCops, 6 to 0, behind Tommy Savoca's pitching. Jim Sundemeyer, Bob Sutton, and Sam Mellilo were standouts for a Tani's team comprised mainly of Blessed Sacrament High School alumni.

Dan Dwarte's grandslam for the Royals kept them close to first place

Competition to determine the first round winner of the American Division title continued with the Royals and Tectape each on win streaks.

Tectape had a 7 to 0 win record for the second round, and the Royals were unbeaten over six games. Frost Men's Shop took a lead of 3 to 0 over the Royals with Jim Sabia driving in Phil Cavellaro and Mike Immediato. Pitcher Caporale then nubbed a triple to drive in Sabia. Cookie Norberto keyed a royal comeback with several extra base hits. The Royals beat pitcher Ed Effern and his Forresters, 6 to 3.

The 1958 contenders were struggling badly this season. The following week, Pat Dorme of Frost's put on his own batting and pitching show by blanking the Forresters. The Forresters managed only singles by Joe Schuck, John Seiser, and Owen Martin. Dorme also hit two homers off Ed Effern.

Finale For the Fifties

In a surprise twist, a favorite opts to skip a title shot.

59

In the first game of the Industrial Division Playoff, the Gems nipped the Adlers, 3 to 2. Charlie Brewster and Charles Ragone knocked in the runs for the Adlers. Gabe Carino notched the win, Dom Ciardullo picked up the loss.

But it wasn't over. In a series "as close as it gets," the Adlers came back in Game Two to beat the Gems, 4 to 3. Harry Battle hit a base-clearing triple for the Adlers to cap a four-run third inning.

Here came Game Three. This deciding contest for the Adlers and the Gems, took place at Columbus Field. Adlers rocketed three runs in the first inning and added another two in the third. The Gems never caught up as manager Harry Rassersmans tried to instill life into his troops. Dom Bucello of the Adlers drove in three runs and scored twice himself.

The Adlers had proven the surprise of 1959 Season. The unlikely match between Tectape and Adler would determine the city championship. A bigger surprise still was that the Royals, citing another tournament to play, did not participate in the 1959 playoffs. It may have been a disappointment to fans, but clearly the Royals had run out of places to stow all the Twilight championship trophies they had claimed during the decade -- eight out of a possible ten!

While an unmanned Russian Luna-2 Rocket sped toward the moon that September, the last fast-pitch softball games of the decade were taking place in New Rochelle. At that time, few Americans interpolated the possibility of a manned landing on the moon let alone a mechanical exploration. Even fewer people gave Adler Electronics a chance to beat Tectape, one of the more powerful fast-pitch teams of the decade.

Dan Brandon's pitching was the keynote to Tectape's second straight city title as the Tapers breezed to the championship With 10-to-0 and 6-to-2 wins over their opponent. Game One was no contest as Tectape saw star performances from Al Ryder, Billy Telesco, and Dick Meade. No Adler baserunner stepped on first base! It might has well been the moon. For Game Two, Brandon relieved Lee Hollis for the win.

Mario Perri had his second Tectape championship win - two in a row.

A Post Card from a Past Time

Think of this book as a post-card from a past time: Wish you all could be here to share in the fun. It was a blast. Time goes by quicker than a Rush Riley sinker, but it was all worth remembering -- the thrills of wins long ago and the agony of having to hang up your mitt too soon.

Fast-pitch provided New Rochelle with a no-cost, exciting, brand of baseball throughout the fifties. But for many reasons, it relinquished its dominance. The new kid on the block, slow-pitch was truly a "every person's game." It was easy to play and was more action packed with hits. The star-driven fast-pitch version was also a burden for the undermanned recreation staffers who couldn't enforce residency requirements as many teams later loaded rosters with gunslinging ringers.

Over time, women who participated in fast-pitch etched their own icons, like Jennie Finch and Lisa Fernandez. They played with all the emotion of their male counterparts, perhaps more. The skills needed to pitch windmill weren't easy to teach, leading to an eventual decline in available pitching talent. Lastly, a lack of field space became critical with the push for slow pitch as well as the burgeoning of woman's softball. None of these factors,

however, takes anything away from the impact of fast-pitch. It defined the amateur sports landscape of its day with the Twilight League—a place for unforgettable characters, teams and high drama. This book hopes the shared repository of those memories and fun times has been reopened for all to know and experience in some measure.

Every pitch was relevant. Every windmill delivery was an engagement, part of a competition. As played in the 1950's, windmill was an extremely exciting game requiring considerable skills. It was a fan-friendly pastime where the proximity of the batter to pitcher also rendered another connection. Even in the stands you could hear the comments made by the pitcher as well as umpires calls and even have a bird's eye view of a play at home plate. One could see the umpire dust off the corner of the plate with his little whisk broom and hear the chatter from the infielders encouraging the pitcher with phrases like "hum babe" or "settle down." Men's fast pitch softball in New Rochelle may be gone. As expressed in the Buddy Holly song "Not Fade Away," its special memories will not be forgotten or fade away for those who took part in that fabulous era.

Epilogue: A Player's Diary from Cuba

It was under a velvet sky, bathed in a fading coppery tropical light, that a lone prop plane made its buzzing descent into Cuba's Jose Marti International Airport in Havana. It was 1959, and though this tropical paradise was eerily poised for the start of a bitter and grudging Cold War, the atmosphere this day was warm both in climate as well as in local spirit thanks to the haberneros who approached the silver plane, now slowing to a stop, with all the overstated officiousness and animated pomp due of a hastily diplomatic visit whose purpose remained unknown.

As passengers readied to disembark onto the palm-tree-lined airfield, alongside a row of squat buildings that pathetically passed for a main terminal, a step ladder was brought alongside the vessel's exit.

These particular passengers were not among the cadre of the KGB advisers and Soviet engineers who were already covertly, though regularly, arriving on the isle to strengthen ties with the likes of Fidel Castro and fans of Che Guevera.

That said, the tobacco capital of the world still remained officially friendly in those days even as Castro's forces were in their final stages of consolidating power. Red, White and Blue banderas adorned with a single star marked a friendly welcome for these unexpected guests. "Esta' Yanquis!," one habanero remarked, leaving some of his comrades puzzling. No, it wasn't the vanguard of some American invasion force as some islanders had actually come to fear due to increasingly strained international relations and political instability.

A question remained. Who exactly were these arrivals? Were these merely "Yanquis," the generic Cuban slang for Nord Americanos? Or, were these the actual heirs of the house that Ruth himself built, the pin-striped New York Yankees?

No one seemed to know.

Adding to the confusion was the fact these English-speaking Yanquis were in fact baseball players, laden with mitts, bats and gear.

Epilogue: Our Yanquis in Cienfuego

Indeed they had come from afar to play ball in this most exotic locale. And if they weren't quick to set the record straight, who could blame these young men for capitalizing on their sudden popularity.

These particular Yankees were members of an All-Star team assembled in New York's Westchester County.

Known at home as "Twilight Leaguers," they heralded from cities with names like New Rochelle, Mount Vernon and Yonkers that formed the northernmost geographical ring of the Big Apple. Others came from even smaller towns like Pelham, Eastchester and Mamaroneck. And unlike the real Yanks these particular Yanquis were mere local legends. Still, Twilighters were amiable amateurs in the best sense of the term – they played America's past-time with dedication and with unrivaled fervor and sportsmanship, all for love of the game rather than for money or hopes of Big League glory.

The kudos that brought them this far from home was as well deserved in 1959, though it would be largely forgotten by official history for some time. They were not just athletes, but artful practitioners of a brand of baseball often overlooked by sports historians – fast-pitch softball. Today many conflate the term "softball" with what was then known as "slow-pitch" softball. They go on to imagine a game where a giant hot-air balloon floats toward the plate at slow motion-speed before it is handily knocked into orbit like Sputnik. That's not what we are talking about. Fast-pitch softball as played by members of the Twilight League was sport where pitching usually was the deciding factor in any matchup and where a handful of artful practitioners could deliver stunning no-hitters with skill and impossible vigor that to the untrained eye might seem a like a theatrical stunts on a level with the type of antics later performed by the Harlem Globetrotters.

Cuban sportsmen in 1959 needed no introduction to the art of windmill.

Used to playing traditional hardball, Cubans also enjoyed this variation of windmill baseball, known locally as "molino vicnto".

And when the Cubans were scouring for the best competition, they looked north.

Championship Matchups of the 1950s
Twilight League

Year	Teams			Champion
1959	Tectape	vs	Adler's	Tectape
1958	Tectape	vs	Forresters	Tectape
1957	Royals	vs	Popeye 9	Royals
1956	Royals	vs	Tectape	Royals
1955	Royals	vs	Tectape	Royals
1954	Royals	vs	Tectape	Royals
1953	Royals	vs	Tectape	Royals
1952	Royals	vs	Gotti 9	Royals
1951	Royals	vs	Empire	Royals
1950	Royals	vs	Bonefro	Royals

Royals used the name "Trotters " in 1953

PARTIAL LIST OF TEAMS OF THE TWILIGHT LEAGUE 1950-59

A
ADLERS

B
BONEFRO CLUB
BOWL-O-RAMA
BLUEBIRDS
BLACK CATS

C
CURLERS
CITY PARK
CALABRIA
CAPPY'S
CHOPPERS
CARLS

D
DARTS
DARCHE 9

E
EMPIRE
EMISA
ECHO BAY

F
FROSTS MENS SHOP
FEENEY PARK BC
FIREMEN
FORRESTERS
FORT SLOCUM

G
GRIES
GRC
GEMS
GOTTI 9
GAY DOME

H
HILITE PHOTO

J
JESTERS
JEEPS
JAYVEES

K
KNIGHTS

L
LOOPERS
LUCKY 9
LEGION

N
NOMADS

O
OUTLAWS
ORIOLES
ORCHIDS

P
POPEYE 9
POLICE
PK'S
PARIS ROGUES
PARIS SHOP

R
ROYALS
RED EYE
ROBINS
RANGERS

S
SCORPIONS
SPARTANS
SPLICERS
SOUTH SIDE BC
SNAPPLE

T
TECTAPE
TMC
TOMPKINS
TROTTERS
TALCO
TEEVEES

U
UNITED
UPSETTERS

V
VETERANS

W
WANAQUE AC
WARRENS
WASHINGTON AC
WHIRLS

554

Edwards Brothers Malloy
Thorofare, NJ USA
December 31, 2013